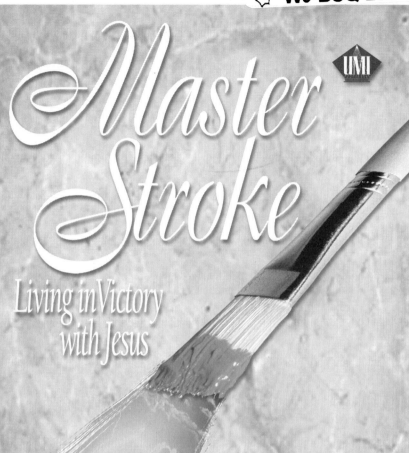

Master Stroke

Living in Victory with Jesus

A. Okechukwu Ogbonnaya, Ph.D.

Publisher
Urban Ministries, Inc.
P.O. Box 436987
Chicago, IL 60643-6987
1.800.860.8642

First Edition
First Printing
ISBN: 0-940955-68-7
Catalog No. 6-5310

*To my love
Benedicta Chinyere Ogbonnaya,
thanks for teaching me how
to live victoriously.*

Other books by the author from Urban Ministries, Inc.:
On Communitarian Divinity
In Step With the Master
Celebrate the Gospel of Jesus
Upon This Rock
Precepts for Living: Annual Sunday School Commentary

TABLE OF CONTENTS

CHAPTER

Introduction

Master Stroke is a compilation of studies dealing with lessons on victories which are afforded to us by the Lord Jesus Christ. We are being called to enter the victory embodied in the person of our Lord. The birth of the Lord in itself announced the victory of our God over the power of the world. The song of the angels at His birth announced our divine instrumentality of victory in the coming world. For those of us who have been living in defeat, this work encourages you to believe that you can move from your defeat to victory through the Lord Jesus Christ. To respond to the voice of Jesus is to respond to the Good News that brings victory. We call you to celebrate the victory—Jesus' birth and the Good News of His forgiveness. As we study, we are being led into the rhythm of joy that may have accomplished His teaching and His action. Yes, even in His death, we see our victory. Because of His suffering, we can finally have victory over the prison of guilt and shame.

We invite you to follow as we look into the life of Jesus as He narrates a parable of victory where a young man moves from the dumps to divine victory. We further invite you to experience Jesus as He gives victory over grief and to see the celebration of the comforted as they accept the offer of His victorious presence. For those who may feel that victory is for the strong because the context of historical existential despair has burdened you, who are living with a weight of pain that makes it hard for you to celebrate—know that Jesus can give you the victory. Are you wondering how to begin walking in the victory which God has already provided for you?

In chapter 5 we study the steps on the way to victory. In chapter 6 there is a lesson in victorious living to be learned from the life Joseph. If your history is filled with betrayals and various pathologies, God can bring you out as He brought Joseph out. He can indeed give you victory.

The privilege of walking in victory with the God of the universe should excite us. Some may marginalize or place barriers between you and God and others around you, thus causing you to believe that you are predestined for defeat, but in these lessons we assure you that victory is yours through Jesus the Messiah. We invite you to experience His victory, to break out of oppression with the power of God which has been made available to you. When life seems ready to crush you under its heavy weight, you can experience the power of the living Lord. When your battles are coming faster than you can think, we want you to know that Jesus has already won the victory for you. Can you walk in it? It is like the sun that rises without you trying to turn it on. All you need to do is acknowledge it and walk in it. You may not know how the provision of victory works, in all its divine mysteries and intricacies, but thank God for it and begin to walk in it.

You see, as children of God, we are victorious beings wearing the badge of honor which is Christ's. But shall we believe God who says that our we have the power to live in victory, or shall we believe the idols of this world who think we are yet without power? The night will fall. When the night time of the soul falls upon your weary soul, hear the Lord as He says, "I am the light of the world." Here is the Good News. Here we are called to enter into the victory of Jesus' life, death and resurrection. Here we are called to speak with Paul, "Yea, but in all this we are more than conquerors." Oh, that we knew and walked in our victory which is already won.

Hopefully, this work will minister to you and encourage you to embrace the victory God has for you. Stop trying to repeat the battle. The Lord our God is mighty in battle and has already given us the victory through the Son, Jesus the Christ, praise be to His name. In the final analysis the goal is for God's children to live out the victorious life in this world, achieve the salvation of the lost, and render ultimate glory to the Lord God and Father of our Savior, Jesus the Christ.

A. Okechukwu Ogbonnaya
Chicago 2001

Chapter One

ANNOUNCING VICTORY

BASED ON MATTHEW 1:18-25

Matthew 1:18-25

Now the birth of Jesus Christ was on this wise: When as his mother Mary was espoused to Joseph, before they came together, she was found with child of the Holy Ghost. ¹⁹ Then Joseph her husband, being a just man, and not willing to make her a public example, was minded to put her away privily. ²⁰ But while he thought on these things, behold, the angel of the Lord appeared unto him in a dream, saying, Joseph, thou son of David, fear not to take unto thee Mary thy wife: for that which is conceived in her is of the Holy Ghost. ²¹ And she shall bring forth a son, and thou shalt call his name JESUS: for he shall save his people from their sins. ²² Now all this was done, that it might be fulfilled which was spoken of the Lord by the prophet, saying, ²³ Behold, a virgin shall be with child, and shall bring forth a son, and they shall call his name Emmanuel, which being interpreted is, God with us. ²⁴ Then Joseph being raised from sleep did as the angel of the Lord had bidden him, and took unto him his wife: ²⁵ And knew her not till she had brought forth her firstborn son: and he called his name JESUS.

Since the fall of Adam and Eve, billions have been born on planet Earth. Born into different cultures, speaking different languages, with different skin tones, each new bundle of joy has been personally created by God (Psalm 139:13) to be a totally unique individual. However, there is *one* thing that we all share in common. Each child born into this fallen world carries the hope of overcoming our downward spiral. No matter what culture or race, each new child carries the possibility of human victory over our spiritual nemesis. Though every baby is born estranged from God, because of the fall of our Edenic ancestors, each child still carries divine possibility. Each baby inherits a sin nature that is a reminder of Adam's children's need for reconciliation with God, other human beings and the environment; and at the same time, each newborn child signals the potential victory of humanity which can begin anew with God.

From Eve's exclamation, "I have received a man (champion) from the Lord" (Genesis 3:1) to the birth of any child today, there is a reminder that humanity needs a champion. We need someone who will lead us into victory over the forces and futilities that have bound us thus far. How can we gain victory over ourselves? How can we be victorious over the powers that have held us down for so long? How can we be saved? From whence would our deliverer come? Who can stand as champion against the principalities and powers of evil in high places that are arrayed against us? Before supposing that these questions are mere philosophical abstractions, let me ask them in another way. What will a sister do whose child is addicted to the chemicals of death that are strewn on the pathways of her children? How can a brother lost in self-pity regain the strength and freedom held captive in the jaws of the lions of the concrete jungle? How can that one whose only friend seems to be the bottle escape to find self-realization? Where can one find the victory? Even more fundamentally, is there power somewhere?

About 2,000 years ago, God embarked on a plan to bring us victory. God's plan has always been to lift fallen humanity up and to bring people back into a divine relationship. The announcement of the presence of Jesus to Joseph portends God's intention to birth a community of victorious people who will follow the victor who now is coming into the world. The story is an announcement of the birth of the victorious one who is God Himself entering the world as human. The Lord is entering the battlefield as a baby. The Creator is approaching as the created. As John puts it, "The true light that gives light to every man was coming into the world" (John 1:9, NIV).

The writer of the text quoted above does not try to hide the fact that this victor has several problems to overcome as He enters into the world. First, He must obtain victory over the circumstances of His conception (Matthew 1:18-19). Second, He must overcome the reluctance of His earthly father. Third, He must gain victory over the suspicion of the woman who carries Him. Fourth, He must gain victory over the human tendency to be judgmental and not just. Fifth, He must gain victory over the law by an outpouring of grace. To do this, an angel of the Lord enters into the dream of Joseph, who was bound by tradition and law. Joseph's obedience to the commands of the angel of the Lord is an important factor in this saga of victory's announcement (vv. 22-25).

The first chapter of Matthew establishes Jesus as the rightful heir to the throne of Israel and the throne of heaven, and therefore as the champion of His people. As David was the champion who delivered the people from the giant Goliath, so will his seed Jesus be our champion in the presence of every Giant we may face in our daily life. We read that Saul killed his thousands and David his ten thousands (1 Samuel 18:7), but not even David's ten thousands can compare with the enemy whom this One entering the world will vanquish through His life and death.

Anyone looked upon as champion of Israel and hence of the world, had to meet two requirements: first, one had to be a descendant of David; second, one had to be a descendant of Abraham. The very first sentence in the Book of Matthew makes the case for Jesus' claim to the throne: "The book of the generation of Jesus Christ, the son of David, the son of Abraham." This announcement is also a victory over sexism, that is the former exclusion of women from the things of God. Jesus' genealogy, which is part of the announcement of Matthew, is unique because it names women among His ancestors. In the patriarchal (male-dominated) society of ancient Israel, this was a very uncommon practice, yet four women are mentioned in the genealogy of our Lord. It is noteworthy that three of them are Black (Tamar: v. 3, Rahab: v. 5, and Bathsheba, the wife of Uriah: v. 6). But to single them out as Black is to obscure the fact that the original Israelites were dark-skinned people and not White.

The victory announced in the Gospel of Matthew is the victory over biological processes. Matthew begins by describing how the birth of Jesus took place. Mary, the mother of Jesus, was engaged to a man named Joseph, but before they were actually married, Mary became pregnant by the power of the Holy Spirit. The account clearly states that there was no human male involved in the birth of Jesus. This is very important because it points to the fact that Jesus Christ was free of the sin nature inherited from Adam and passed on through the generations by the male. If Jesus had been conceived as any other baby, it would be extremely difficult to believe that He is God. It was necessary for Jesus to be born of a human mother and a divine Father. He had to be conceived of the Holy Spirit so that He could be Emmanuel—God with us—who came to "save His people from their sins" (Matthew 1:21). He now lives forever as the eternal God-Man. Because Jesus walked the earth as a man, He can identify with all of our trials and temptations. Because He reigns in heaven as God, He has the power to bring us through our trials and help us overcome our temptations.

Ancient Jewish marriages took place in three stages: First, there was the engagement, which was generally arranged by the couple's parents years before the actual marriage took place. Next came the betrothal where the dowry was settled, and finally, a public announcement was made and the couple was joined by the marriage benediction.

From the moment of betrothal, the relationship was considered as binding as if the couple had actually consummated the marriage. The only way out of the union was a written bill of divorcement. If between the betrothal and the consummation a woman was found not to be a virgin, she could be stoned to death (Deuteronomy 22:20-21). That's why Joseph had determined to "put her away" or privately give Mary a bill of divorcement which said in effect, "This woman is not my wife; I am not her husband." Joseph loved Mary, and even if she had cheated him as he believed, he did not want to expose her to public humiliation and possible death. His actions reveal several things about his character: he was a righteous man (v. 19); he was

responsive to God (v. 24); and he was a man of strong discipline (v. 25).

It took divine intervention to convince Joseph of the divine conception. God had to enter a dream to make Joseph victorious over his own doubt and misgivings. God not only enters Joseph's dream, He also names the child (vv. 20-21). By entering into Joseph's dream, God shows that the divine can penetrate even our deepest thoughts and transform our perception. You see sometimes our dreams are the repository of our anxieties and hidden fears. But even in those deep recesses of our most unsettling dreams, we still feel a tinge of divine hope.

This is not the first time the Lord God entered into the dream of one whom He chose to use for greater purpose. Recall how God entered into the dream of Joseph's ancestral namesake, changing the course of history for the people of Israel. Remember the experience of his ancestor Jacob who in a dream experienced the opening of heaven and the descending and ascending of angels. Our dreams are avenues for divine entrance into our lives. I am not speaking only of the sleep state where dreams happen but also of the dreams we have while awake–our vision of the future. Our hopes and expectations for the future can transform our hearts into a doorway into eternity. God finds a way into our hearts as we dream. Notice that Joseph's hope was mainly of saving the woman he loved. He wished, dreamed if you will, to deliver her, to save her from the hands of judgment. It is this desire, I believe, that prepared him for the entrance of God. The fact that Joseph sought to save Mary may have created a doorway for him to understand when God said of the child in Mary's womb, "he shall save . . . ."

How does God give Joseph victory over his anxiety? Joseph's dream is an affirmation of what God said to Mary. The Bible does not tell us that Mary told Joseph what the angel had told her. But it is safe to assume that she did. Much more than that, God through His angel affirms the words of the prophet to this worried man. It is upon this confirmation of Mary's story that Joseph got the courage to go ahead with the wedding plans. Not only was there an affirmation of the words of the prophets, but there was an affirmation of Joseph's identity. The angel addressed Joseph as "son of David." This was a princely title and spoke not only to Joseph's being a descendant of David, but also to the esteem he was about to receive—the honor of being the guardian of the promised Messiah. Oh, how this affirmation must have spoken to the heart of Joseph!

Divine affirmation is a pathway to human victory. When we reach those moments when our soul must struggle with right versus right; when it seems that the divine is speaking with two voices both of which are right; when our heart is torn with anxiety because the right we must do will hurt the ones that we love;

when our very good threatens to undo our faith; and when our dreams turn to nightmares and we question the very landscape on which God has so securely planted us, it is then that God comes with a new dream—a dream of the possibility of victory, a dream in which divine affirmations undo all that denies our wholeness.

There are some of you reading this now who are caught between bad and good. Or caught between love and pain, or between a vision and a nightmare. Let me assure you that God delights to enter into your dreams—as anxiety-filled as they may be—and when God comes, He will bring with Him divine affirmation. The God who said "be anxious for nothing" is ready to give you reason to trust. And that reason is the gift of Himself—total and complete.

But this affirmation was not grounded merely in Joseph's dream of God. It would take more than that to draw victory from a cowering heart. It would take more than the birth of another child into this world to save us from sin. For many children have been born with the promise of deliverance and have themselves fallen victim to the very problems which they were supposedly meant to have victory over. The signal for the victory was evident in the name of Jesus. The name itself is a song of God's promise of victory for the people.

The name of Jesus spoke to the act of God in the salvation of His people. Many people had been given that name prior to the birth of Jesus of Nazareth, their name could not grant the victory that this one could. The angel told Joseph the child would be a male who would be called Jesus. In this amazing announcement, the angel does not leave salvation as an amorphous unfocused reality, but instead tells specifically what this child named Jesus would give victory over: "He will save His people from their sins" (v. 21). Jesus will give victory over the power of sin.

"Jesus" is the Greek form of the Hebrew *Yeshua* meaning "Jehovah is Salvation." The principal reason Jesus came to earth is to gain victory over sin so that humanity would no longer have to be slaves to sin. Jesus is our Saviour, victory over our human condition and our evil archenemy is impossible without Him.

14

"Neither is there salvation in any other: for there is none other name given among men whereby we must be saved" (Acts 4:12). "Jesus" was a common name among the ancient Israelites, but Mary's baby was called "Jesus the *Messiah*." We inherited the Greek title "Christ," which we use often instead of the Hebrew word Messiah meaning the "Anointed One." It must be remembered that many were called Christ, particularly, the judges who gave the people victory over their enemies. However, Jesus came to do battle with our archenemy, Satan.

Even before His birth, Jesus defeated the devices of the enemy in the life of Joseph and brought about victory. But here the writer declares that this one enemy who has felled every human being—this one enemy that is at the root of all human failure, this bane of human heartache, this shackle of iron that has caused the capitulation of even the most pristine of human souls, this father of the restlessness and of waywardness driven deep into the human psyche—now has met its match. Is Jesus, who has blood like our blood and bone like our bones, enough to grant us victory over this corrupting captor of our souls? Can this really be? Can this purveyor of human heartache have met its match? Oh, yes! The angel says "He shall save his people from their sins."

To understand the extent of this victory we need to summarize the nature of sin here briefly. At the heart of all the fear and the corruption; at the center of all the absence of mercy and justice; in the eye of the storm of the lack of compassion so prevalent in our world is that three-letter word: SIN. The Bible uses different terminology to describe this cancer of the human soul. This growth that chokes the life out of the spirit of human beings, without any possibility of understatement, sin is the most stubborn problem that humanity faces. It is sin that led Paul to cry "O wretched man that I am" (Romans 7:24). It is the experience of sin that led David to bewail "behold I was brought forth in iniquity and in sin did my mother conceive me" (Psalm 51:5). Sin led Adam to flee from God's presence and pulled his descendants out of Eden. To understand the importance of the statement "he shall save his people from their sins," one needs to grasp the extensive nature of sin. Job 14:4 asks, "Who can bring a clean thing out of an unclean?" and with exclamation answers, "No one!" There has never been a human being who was unaffected by what this three-letter word represents.

The terminologies used for sin also point out its extensive nature. The word used here is "harmation," which means hitting the wrong target (John 1:29; 8:21; 8:24; 1 John 1:10). It is also referred to as a worthless act in the New Testament from the Greek *poneros* (John 3:19; 17:15); it is referred to as unrighteousness by the use of the Greek word *adikia* denoting actions by which humans rebel against God, miss His purpose for their life, and surrender to the power of evil rather than to God. Sin points to our inner rebellion against God. This rebellion is present even when we put on a religious facade. Humanity's estrangement from God, is based in this inner rebellion.

It is Jesus, as the angels foretold, who will save human beings from sin. He will be victor over the external as well as the internal shackles of slavery to sin. Jesus has the capacity to conquer through love without destroying us in whom sin is so deeply ingrained. That is a great love, for you see we all have sinned, without exception we are dominated by this three-letter word (Romans 3:9-23). And because every sin is against God, to gain the victory for us, Jesus must stand between us and the One whom we have offended. Only He can save us when what we have been and done has been in direct violation of God's righteousness.

The Gospel of Matthew enables us to see the child who is coming not merely from a human perspective, for it begins by telling us that this child is born of the Holy Spirit. That makes the child unique. Because he is Jewish, Joseph would probably accept the circumstance of such a birth. Many, including Isaac and Samson have been born by the power of the most high. So the angel made sure that Joseph understood that Jesus' entrance into the world would bring victory. He says that this One who will be born is God intervening into human existence. This is God seeking to extricate us from the chains which have gripped our soul. He tells us that this One who will give us victory is Emmanuel—God with us.

Note that the angel does not say God *is* with us. That simply leads to the often repeated idea that God's presence is with us. But here is *God with us,* not through His messenger or through some feeling, but in the very divine essence as a historical being in our midst. This victory is possible because God comes down from heaven and dwells with us. God comes here to earth and does battle for us in the person of the Messiah, Jesus.

This Jesus is the One who had been predicted by prophets from Moses to Malachi. This Jesus would save us from our sins by personally paying the penalty of sin on our behalf, offering Himself as our eternal sacrifice. This truth makes Christianity unique from all other religions of the world. Unlike the false gods of other religions, our God came not only to make bad people good, but to make dead people live. How awesome that God came down to save us! That He would do battle with our mortal enemy to give His victory to us as a free gift.

The heart of Joseph must have leapt in the proclamation of victory, and he was likely moved to act with confidence. Many who have understood this victorious message have become emboldened in the face of evil yet humbled by the depth of God's love. To be clear about the victory that Jesus came to give; to be clear that God came not just as some terrestrial messenger, as awesome as that may be, makes one not only want to shout from the mountain top but releases in one the courage to be and to act to the end that one might participate in that victory. Yet, many still walk in defeat who should know this gift of divine victory. Oh that God will open our eyes to see this victory bought by *God with us.* "He shall save his people from their sins." That spells victory. Not mine, not yours, but God's. It is a gift wrapped in a baby. Divine victory is so simply and profoundly given. When we come to know it, we cannot help but be moved.

God's revelation of the coming victory through the Messiah gave Joseph the power to be obedient to the word of God (vv. 22-25). Joseph is an excellent example of total obedience to God. At the instruction of an angel, he changed his plans and married the pregnant Mary. His family was probably outraged and disgraced. His friends probably advised him against marrying a woman who had gotten pregnant by someone else while betrothed to him. But Joseph knew what he had heard from God, and the strength of his character was measured by how much he was willing to suffer to do what was right. Because of his obedience to God, Joseph was given the incredible honor of nurturing and protecting the promised Christ Child. His integrity enabled him to spend years of private time in the presence of Emmanuel, "God with us." He listened to God and saved Jesus from death at the hands of Herod's soldiers. Joseph was a very religious man. However, it was not his religion but his obedience for which he is remembered. Samuel, the prophet, told King Saul that "to obey is better than sacrifice" (1 Samuel 15:22, paraphrased). Religious ritual should be a physical demonstration of a right relationship with God. Being religious (going to church, singing in the choir, serving on committees) is useful and beautiful when we are motivated by love and obedience to God.

Jesus as Emmanuel—God with us is the one who proclaims within us a bent toward victory rather than a bent to despair. Since this is God coming to take our side, the enemy and the spiritual forces arrayed against us cannot stand before us. There is an immediate victory because God is immediately present. Understand that Jesus is the Mediator between God and human beings, but also remember that He, being the Messiah, is God and as God He is that to which He mediates. Thus in His presence we need no more mediation for He is the very One to whom we resort and the One who bears us to the center of divinity where He Himself exists. Only God can bring us to God. He is more than a connection, He is the life-line, He is more than a ladder, He is the One by whom we ascend. He is more than a pathway, He is the way we must walk. We have relationship with God because God Himself is with us. Because God is with us, there is evidence that God is effective in our lives, healing and drawing us to His righteousness and lifting us into previously unknown realms of spiritual power and victory.

Victory is announced over our fears of human conquest, over our false religious idols, and over our self-righteousness and judgmental posture. This victorious announcement leads into a flow of mercy. The announcement about Jesus to Joseph is an announcement of the possibility of victory over all angst about the approval and disapproval of people. His very life validates our connection with God. Jesus saves our future and reestablishes our relationship with divinity. He is the language of God's victorious heart. Victory becomes real through the movement of the renewing presence of Jesus. It is the presence of Jesus that allows us to transcend the line of demarcation between a defeated life and a victorious life and opens to us the possibility of victory everlasting.

This victory allows us to speak a new language. But it is not enough to speak a new language or even join a new church. There must be a new way of seeing and being grounded in the fact that God is with us, and understanding the importance and implications of this revelation. He is not only with us, for one can be with you and not for you. This is not a letter-writing God who is far away as noted in the theology which argued that God is living in a foreign land and has sent a love letter yet His presence is just a distant memory. We must state that God is not just with us—but also for us. Indeed, God is with us and is for us, therefore who can be against us? (Romans 8)

Jesus came into the world to define a new relationship between us and God, between us and each other, and between us and the world we live in. But given the mess in which we find ourselves, He came in ready to fight and to give His life for us. Our challenge is beyond all human methodologies-seeking God, seeking the divine. Our search is not for a technique or a gimmick, but a personal entrance into a relationship with God. To reduce our desire for God to a methodology is to distort the significance of the divine mystery. To reduce God's divine love and willingness to be in relation with us to a nice idea is philistine and irreverent. The critical part in this God-with–us-ness is the recognition that divine reality, has willingly entered with us into the material realm and experience. This is what one may call divine praxis (learning)—structuring human life by entering into it intentionally in order to transform it. That transformational entrance of God into the world has a purpose. That purpose is for us who have seen Him to participate in His power and thereby become victorious.

In our text, Mary gains victory over physical constraints. Mary was a virgin and, as such, was physically unable to procreate. Science says that a woman cannot have a baby without the help of a man, whether through sexual intercourse or through artificial insemination. As human beings, we are often caught in situations where we seem to be entrapped by our physical limitations. Some may be born with physical disabilities, others may inherit a genetic defect from their parents, while others may suffer from chronic illness. God takes the extreme case of physical limitations and shows us that we can have victory over them. In this story, God breaks the physical law. He shows His power even over physical and biological limitations. This miracle signals that we are being prepared to overcome all the physical obstacles that may stand in our way. Your physical situation is not a hindrance to God.

This announcement of divine victory is also a victory over fear. Joseph was afraid of the consequences of broken tradition. He was afraid for himself, as well as for Mary. Fear often prevents us from thinking clearly. However, God gives Joseph victory over the fear that so gripped him that he was willing to let Mary go. The reality is that Mary would still be in danger even if he put her away privately as he intended. The law would have demanded that Mary point out the father of the child, and if she could not she would have been stoned to death. The question remained: was Mary safer away from Joseph or was she safer with Joseph? The fact is that her safety lay only with Joseph. Joseph was afraid the people would shame the woman he loved. His fear grew out of Jewish tradition and legalism. We must take courage from the fact that God did not sit on the sidelines, but entered actively into the situation. In fact, God entered into Joseph's consciousness to help him gain enough confidence to walk in divine victory.

The intent of divine entrance into our lives is to encourage us to participate in God's plan and appropriate His power so that we can promote God's reign in this world. By coming into the world, Jesus uncovers the negative structures of our consciousness and reveals how our false interpretation of righteousness and our fears keep us in bondage and may in fact lead us to endanger the very lives and salvation of others. The enemy plays on our religious sensibilities; he can take our care and turn it against us. But thank God that He enters into our situation and speaks clearly to us. Jesus came into the world not just to uncover our negative structures, but also to help us discover God's goodness toward us.

Only God can breathe new life, plant an uncorrupt seed, and develop within us new life and a new way of living in the world that leads to wholeness. This is what the announcement of victory here means: that God as incarnate in Jesus Christ (Yeshua Messiah) reconciles the world to Himself. Thanks be to God who gives us the victory through Jesus Christ our Lord.

Chapter Two

FROM DEFEAT TO VICTORY
BASED ON LUKE 15:1-2, 11-24

Luke 15:1-2

Then drew near unto him all the publicans and sinners for to hear him. ² *And the Pharisees and scribes murmured, saying, This man receiveth sinners, and eateth with them.*

Luke 15:11-24

And he said, A certain man had two sons: ¹² *And the younger of them said to his father, Father, give me the portion of goods that falleth to me. And he divided unto them his living.* ¹³ *And not many days after the younger son gathered all together, and took his journey into a far country, and there wasted his substance with riotous living.* ¹⁴ *And when he had spent all, there arose a mighty famine in that land; and he began to be in want.* ¹⁵ *And he went and joined himself to a citizen of that country; and he sent him into his fields to feed swine.* ¹⁶ *And he would fain have filled his belly with the husks that the swine did eat: and no man gave unto him.* ¹⁷ *And when he came to himself, he said, How many hired servants of my father's have bread enough and to spare, and I perish with hunger!* ¹⁸ *I will arise and go to my father, and will say unto him, Father, I have sinned against heaven, and before thee,* ¹⁹ *And am no more worthy to be called thy son: make me as one of thy hired servants.* ²⁰ *And he arose, and came to his father. But when he was yet a great way off, his father saw him, and had compassion, and ran, and fell on his neck, and kissed him.* ²¹ *And the son said unto him, Father, I have sinned against heaven, and in thy sight, and am no more worthy to be called thy son.* ²² *But the father said to his servants, Bring forth the best robe, and put it on him; and put a ring on his hand, and shoes on his feet:* ²³ *And bring hither the fatted calf, and kill it; and let us eat, and be merry:* ²⁴ *For this my son was dead, and is alive again; he was lost, and is found. And they began to be merry.*

The key verse in this entire Scripture passage is, "For this my son was dead, and is alive again; he was lost, and is found. And they began to be merry" (Luke 15:24). Is this not the problem that lies at the very heart of the human condition? Is not our problem the fact that we are living in the presence of death? Not only do we live in the presence of physical death, but we also live in the presence of spiritual decay. Even within the church one can see what Freud called *thanatos*—the principle of death at work. While I believe that Freud was wrong in his analysis of religion, I cannot help but point out the validity of his insight into what he called the human death wish. He probably never knew how close he was to the biblical assessment of the human condition. Jesus Himself, in describing our world says, "and this is the condemnation, that the light has come into the world, and men loved darkness rather than the light, because their deeds were evil" (John 3:19).

Too often, the children of God venture out from Him to try exactly the kind of things we are ashamed to talk about among God's people. Sometimes we do things just because the money will be good. We may sometimes decide that what we are about to do, even though the Holy Spirit raises loud objections, is worth the risk. Freud called this the death wish. The truth is that once we get into some of the things we crave, we discover that they may put us in regular association with people whose world views are antithetical to that in which the Spirit of God has instructed us. In fact, this death wish leads some of us to get involved with others with destructive behaviors or as we say "downright sleazy folks." Soon we find ourselves waging wars that our spiritually depleted armory has nothing left to fight with. Some of us return to old habits hoping to rekindle the pleasures these vanities once provided for us. If not rescued by the grace of God, we plunge deeper and deeper into new forms of addictive behavior to drown out our screeching conscience which by this time is in overdrive trying to veer us off into the wide path to self-destruction.

When we get caught in this maze of contradiction and entangled by the tentacles of the spiritual death wish, we cease to hear what others may be saying. We even claim that our behavior is a personal choice, though our ability to choose has long been vanquished by the commitment to self-destruction. Some of us drop out of church. Others of us continue to attend despite the fact that "people may be buzzing"; we still get dressed for church and in fact talk church talk. All through this, God will continue to speak to us. Even through the "buzzing" of people, God may still be speaking to us. We may feel victimized even though we are in the wrong and conclude that this is due to the hypocrisy of the people at the church. The pastor's message is perceived as judgmental and intrusive. However, the key to overcoming this bent to self-destruction laced with self-deception is to acknowledge that God knows all our business anyway. God will reach us by all the means at His disposal—for it is not the will of God that any of us will perish. Unfortunately, sometimes God must reach us by a head-on collision.

The story of the prodigal son is more than just the story of a rebellious child leaving his home and family. It is more than the story of a sinner leaving God. It is the story of coming to oneself, a story of the rekindling of consciousness and the transforming power of divine memory. The wayward son remembered his father's house as a means of victorious living. It reveals the free acceptance and redemption which seals our victory over our own waywardness and affirms our inclusion into the Father's house based on grace and love. Our victory is undergirded by divine grace, mercy, and love. The story is told by Jesus to show how both runaway sinners and judgmental saints gain victory over their conditions. Both need the Master Stroke of divine mercy. Both must move from being victimized to living in the victory which God provides.

The first group of people who appear in this story are Pharisees and scribes. These people disapproved Jesus' interaction with those who were not in the "in crowd," who were less worthy of religious favors than others (Luke 15:1-2). The Pharisees and scribes criticized Jesus for His open fraternization with publicans and sinners. Jesus socialized with those whom Israel rejected. His free association with them threatened the very foundation on which the pious stood. Publicans, or tax collectors, and sinners were considered to be unclean. The publicans had given themselves over to be used by the Roman government to collect taxes from their own oppressed compatriots. Sinners were those who failed to adhere strictly to the Law. By contrast, the Pharisees and scribes considered themselves to be among the most holy. While these groups did not go out and sin deliberately and seek to deny God explicitly, they were also subject to the death principle for they were not consumed with concern for those who were outside of their joyride to heaven.

How can I call these religious leaders, these pastors, deacons, and elders subjects of the death wish principle? You see, while they knew God and knew that God intended for sinners to live (Ezekiel), they stood in the way of all who sought to draw these people away from the death and destruction to which they were so accustomed. How could these religious leaders who had all this knowledge fault Jesus for associating with the marginalized and the fallen? Looking at the Pharisees and scribes one cannot help but wonder if they did not dress up on the Sabbath, walk to church, and pass by the same people that Jesus was fraternizing with, who caused them so much anger.

I wonder if they sang the songs of Zion which spoke of God's love for all creation while they complained about ministers who would reach the outcast. Similarly, I wonder how modern-day churches can thrive but have little effect on their surrounding neighborhoods. I wonder how members of the church can close the door to the poor and needy who sit, walk, stand, and sometimes sleep at the doorstep of the church. It is this principle of the death wish which makes church people value money more than ministry, silver more than salvation, show more than souls, and sometimes gold more than God.

While Jesus, in the story of the prodigal son, was explicitly speaking of people who are swimming in the mud with pigs, He nonetheless was speaking to the pigs' friends in the temple whose attitude toward their dying brothers and sisters was nothing less than piggish. When we watch while souls perish, when we pile up money and things while others suffer, when we sing praises to God while ignoring the least of these, are we not piggish and co-opted by the death principle? When we fight about explicit injunctions of Scripture in order to gain acceptance for what God condemns, are we not really among those who favor the death principle?

The scribes and Pharisees believed that association with these transgressors of the Law would contaminate them. They would not even associate with them, let alone eat with them. Sharing a meal together would indicate that they considered them candidates for salvation. Eating is a sign of friendship. By eating with the outcasts Jesus had chosen them as friends. The English word "companion" is derived from the word *com-panis,* meaning "with bread." Their faulty logic which is also common today was that entering into the company of sinners was to share their character.

As we know, it was common for Jesus to eat with sinners. Those of us who are believers will readily agree that Jesus was clearly not a sinner. Yet He chose to ignore religious and social convention to associate with them as a means of bringing God's News to them. Jesus chose to associate with the outcasts over acceptable church folk. But people who are part of the death principle cannot see their way clearly enough to touch those who are outside. That is why I find it difficult to accept the belief that Christians should not fraternize with a certain kind of people. Jesus Himself provides an example which calls us beyond those who are acceptable to us or those who share our religious sensibilities. He calls us to reach out to all whom we may be instrumental in shining the light of the Messiah into their situation, thereby transforming their lives.

It is to that group of religious people with a death wish for the outcast that Jesus tells this parable. In their unrighteous indignation and bias against the poor of Israel, they questioned Jesus' integrity. Their discriminatory attitudes moved Jesus to tell three parables. He wanted to teach them that no one was hopeless in the eyes of God and that one who was cast down could find his way to victorious living by the power of God's unconditional love.

This parable is not just about those who have left the master's house and seem to have lost their capacity for redemption, but the possibility for redeeming those who were inside and were lost as well. Through the parable of the prodigal, Jesus shows that those who are involved in the things of God have many spiritual difficulties which they must recognize and for which they must seek the victory of God. While Jesus did not wait until the down-trodden came to Him, today's church keeps waiting. We preach at them through TV, we write books for them, we speak to them on the radio, we will even pay someone to talk to them, but we will not go to them.

Jesus went to where they were and reached out to them. In those days, the Pharisees sucked in their breath and pulled their robes tightly around them to avoid contamination. Today the church testifies to one another or fights one another and forgets that Jesus freely associated with sinners and calls us to do the same. There is a place for theological discourse, but discourse without deliverance is discord.

Let's delve into the parable by beginning with its context. Prior to telling the story of the wayward son, often referred to as the prodigal son, Jesus told two other parables. The first was about the value of even one lost sheep to the shepherd. The shepherd steps away from 99 sheep that are secured to find the one that has gone astray. When the lost sheep is found, the shepherd rejoices. In the second story, Jesus told the parable of the lost coin. Jesus used this story to explain that every soul is valuable to the kingdom, no matter how many may already be present.

Finally, Jesus told the story of the lost son, something far more valuable than a coin, or even a sheep. When this story is inter-preted in terms of the kingdom, those who are supposed to be in the right may be less pleasing to God than the penitent one who has gone astray. The story of the prodigal son is a vivid rep-resentation of the point Jesus was trying to make with the Pharisees. In this story, the younger of a man's two sons came to his father requesting his inheritance. According to Jewish Law, the younger son was to be allotted one-third of the estate follow-ing the death of his father. Knowing it was within his father's power to abdicate his wealth prior to his death, this young man didn't want to wait any longer. Once the son accepted his portion of the inheritance, he had no further claim on his father's estate or the family possessions. The very nature of the son's request indicates that the younger son possessed a rebellious spirit which could only be quenched through a hard life lesson.

Instead of being a dutiful son, one who honored his father and his mother according to the fifth commandment (Exodus 20:12), this young man went away into a far country. He showed no concern for the welfare of his father in old age. He was driven solely by selfish desires. He left Palestine and went into a Gentile region. The son was not wrong for requesting his share of the inheritance. His transgression was in cutting himself off from his father's love and protection, assuming he could take care of his own needs. Through his actions, the son renounced his status as son. This is also the condition of sinners whom Jesus has called to repentance. They have no claim to the inheritance of eternal life because they are not a part of His family.

Many people search elsewhere for salvation, just as the prodigal went elsewhere seeking what he thought would make him happy. Because he cut himself off from his father, the prodigal now had to rely on his own resources. He squandered his inheritance quickly. He gave no thought to planning for his future and disposed of all he had through riotous living. He did not anticipate that a day of trouble would come in the form of a mighty famine. Fear and panic likely prevailed as everyone was probably having a hard time during the period of famine.

The prodigal son had made no provisions for his future and had cut himself off from the only one who cared to help him. All he had left now was his own thoughts and the time to assess how and why he had ventured down the wrong path. He left home seeking the thrills that he thought life had to offer. Instead, he found the hard truths of life when away from the safety and security of his father's home. The loss of his money and friends gave him an opportunity to think about his self-centered choices.

Things got so bad that he was forced into the most disgusting form of employment a Jew could undertake—feeding swine. Leviticus 11:8 reveals the Jewish attitude toward swine: "Of their flesh shall ye not eat, and their carcass shall ye not touch; they are unclean to you." Swine were not even to be touched by Jews. The young man had left his Jewish home where there was love and abundance only to descend into the worst kind of job, working for a Gentile boss. He got so hungry that he would gladly have eaten the animal's feed: the pods of the carob trees, eaten only by animals and the very poorest humans. He had hit bottom!

Then the prodigal came to himself. It was as though he was able to step outside of himself and see the sorry state he was in. He remembered that he was the son of a wealthy father who had servants and bread enough to spare. He had no need to beg because the father who loved him was wealthy. It is at this point, the parable of the prodigal distinguishes itself from the stories of the lost sheep and the lost coin. Those lost objects had to be found by the initiative of someone. In the case of the prodigal, he could not be found until he desired to be found. He now understood all that he had given up when he renounced his sonship by taking his inheritance and going far away from his father. Now that he was aware of his transgression and his helpless state, he was ready to be found. He decided to return to the land of his father.

The prodigal still used the term "father," although he recognized that he was no longer worthy to be called "son." The prodigal's penitence and humility is demonstrated by his willingness to go home and be a servant in his father's house. He was ready to acknowledge his wrongdoing. Here it is important to recognize that before the son had an opportunity to make his confession, the father had compassion on him; he hugged and kissed him. The prodigal repented and was fully prepared to take whatever the father was willing to give. But the father received his long lost son with joy and open arms.

While the prodigal needed to confess his sinfulness and his unworthiness, the father was more interested in rejoicing over the fact that his son had come home. His return was a cause for celebration. Looking at the prodigal's father as our heavenly Father, all believers can know that once we are prepared to come to Him in humility and repentance, He joyously receives us. In fact, He cannot wait for the opportunity to lavish His love on His wandering children who have returned to Him.

God wants the best for us, just as the prodigal's father wanted the best for his son. He ran to him, stripping off the rags he had worn and exchanging them for a robe worthy of his son. The fatted calf was killed to be eaten as the homecoming celebration. It was time to be merry because the son who was dead was alive again. By telling this parable, Jesus invited the religious men of the day to discard their resentments of the lowly and to join the celebration with Jesus and the other prodigals who had come home to the Father. Later in the parable, the resentment of the older brother parallels the resentment of the Pharisees, but God loves them all equally, the wayward and the devoted.

How did the prodigal get into this condition? First of all let us notice that he was in his fathers' house without lack. In his father's house he was protected and cared for. His every need was met. He had his health and the security of a family that loved him. We know that his father loved him. How do we know that? By the fact that his father was willing to give him part of the inheritance while he was still alive. The father was not obligated to do so; only love and maybe the desire for peace within the household would have led him to do this.

The first slope downward for this man was selfishness. He wanted his father's property which legally did not belong to him. Selfishness tends to breed impatience. He could not wait until the will was executed. He had to have it now or else. How many times has haste led us into trouble? Most haste is grounded in selfishness. In fact, selfishness and the haste which it breeds are contrary to faith and the patience that grows out of it. It is this unbridled desire for immediate satisfaction which often leads not only to impatience and haste for wealth but also to the gambling tables and, for some of our children today, to drug dealing, pimping, cheating and lying. It is this selfishness which fuels the need to get bigger gadgets and newer toys which fail to fill the immense void deepening in our own psychic hades and emotional restlessness.

There was also a touch of rebellion in the demand for his portion of the wealth. How do I know? The text tells that he went off to the Gentiles' lands. He probably wanted to be free from all the restraints which he thought his parents had placed upon him. Like many, he may have thought the godly life was too constricting and that walking with God was best left for those who were ready to see their maker. Could he have been thinking that it is better to enjoy himself while he was young? Like most of us he did not know what tomorrow would bring. Many times children of God are tempted to run with the world, taking the blessing they received while in the house of the Lord to run off to experience the world. "What is the use?" he probably said to himself. "How will all this obedience benefit me?"

So here we find selfishness, haste, and rebellion leading this young man downward. But is he different from us? If he is, are we different from the Pharisees and Saducees or from the brother who stayed but yet was filled with his own inner restlessness, haste, selfishness, and bitterness? But let's continue to examine the prodigal. He moved away from the place where people knew him. This is a refusal to be accountable. He does not move next door to the church where people know him. He moves into a place where he can maintain anonymity. If he lived in our day, he would move into a larger church, move to another city, and change his career with the hope that these moves would mask the rebellion and keep people from knowing his true identity.

Here was a Jewish kid who did not move to be a witness but to waste away. Usually when we begin to desire the forbidden, our selfishness gets hold of us and we want what we want in haste; we rebel against everything and everyone. We wonder if this Jewish young man was ashamed of his rebellious demands and therefore had to leave town. Jesus does not tell us this. But the culture was one of shame and honor. A young man taking such action would have been dishonored and would have had to hide his face. Let's examine ourselves. It is not easy for us to face the shame of our rebellion, neither are we willing to be held accountable for our selfish acts. There is much talk about accountability today, but the truth is that we want to run away—

from the church, from the family, from the city, from friends, and yes, from God. But sometimes it seems that the more we run, the more into trouble we sink.

Note another aspect of this story. He squandered all his assets. The path to defeat is filled with squandered time, squandered opportunity, squandered friendships, squandered relationships, and squandered talents. Instead of waiting on God, we take a chance with fleeting things. We are shocked when these chances turn out to be exactly that—"chances." Having staked his familiar relationship and inheritance on the chance that he might succeed, the prodigal was now in a place of trouble. Not only had he lost his relationships but the material things upon which he placed a high premium were gone.

It is a deeply spiritual problem when we do not realize that things will not replace relationships. This young man had the illusion that material things would replace relationships. But having lost his family relationships he turned to using material things to maintain appearance of friendships. But the problem with material things is that they do have a tendency to slip away and we are left wanting.

When he lost his fair-weather friends, how could he get victory over his situation? We discover that he would hit rock bottom before he reaches up for the hands of victory. We follow this young man in another city where he is penniless, alone, probably sick and unkempt. Jesus tells us that he became a keeper of pigs and was forced to share the grub with the hogs. He wanted to be anonymous and now he truly was where no one would have recognized him who knew him before he set on his road to "freedom." Human beings often wind up in places they thought they wanted to go. However, there is victory even for one who has gone into the deepest pit and to the farthest of ungodly lands. How can one who finds himself or herself in this downward slide receive the victory to overcome? It is important to remember that we need not wait until we are at this point to take a hold of the rope of victory. Victory may be grasped at any point along the downward slide.

Notice the progression. First, "he journeyed to a far country," Second, he "wasted his possessions with prodigal living" (NKJV) by squandering that for which he had control. Our attitude toward control is directly tied to how we respond when faced with situations we cannot control. We read further that third, "there arose a severe famine in the land" which then affected him deeply. "He began to want," which was the fourth step in the progression. At the fifth, we find a young man who now had to look for someone to whom he could attach himself. "He went and joined himself to a citizen of the country," we read. Who knows how he felt as he was forced to relinquish his independence. Rather than bringing him in to form a relationship with him, this man "sent him to the field to feed swine." As the writer approaches a final crescendo one can feel the despairing penultimate note: "and he would have gladly filled his stomach with the pods that the swine ate."

Human pride and human selfishness oftentimes bring us back full circle to wish for what we would have at other times disdained. How pitiful to ignore the blessing of a great benefactor, such as God, to turn up one's nose at the divine gift, to pelt a divine messenger with mud, only to turn around in time of need and wish for that which God had intended and not find it. The ultimate descent into the pit of defeat and despair is heralded as we find the prodigal brought to his lowest point "and no one gave him anything." That parallels the descent of humanity set on a path away from a loving God.

One can imagine as Jesus reached this point of the story that the people held their breath and felt the depth of the fall, some wishing they could save him, others believing he deserved to be brought low, while some were torn. Yet no matter how one feels, one knows that defeat in this case seems final for this prodigal. He is like the addict in our day who has stolen from his father, used his mother, abused his spouse, cheated his friends, disappointed his children, and turned on God. How is victory possible for such a one? Who will deliver him? How shall he return to the place of mercy and new beginning?

The writer of the text has led us, as Dante does, into the inferno, but now summons us to listen to a rising note. A harmonious note is ringing in the distant land of this man's lost consciousness. A divine seed is breaking through ground in the shadowlands of this man's decrepit psychic landscape. The Lord now calls the listeners to know that there is no defeat so complete that it erases the potential for victory. Even in the midst of our groveling with pigs, God sets a course for our return to divine victory. What occurs in the life of this man to bring him back to the house of victory? First, it is implied here that the father never stopped loving this wayward child. It is clear that the father of this young man represents God. It follows then that love—God's love for us—is the foundation of our return to victory. Verses 20 and 22 point out that the love of the father had never ceased. It was this unconditional love, even without his knowledge, which continued to sustain the prodigal even in his waywardness. It is only because of God's unconditional love for us that we have not died. It is by this love that we are able to rise over and over again. How many times have we fallen, been destroyed, or lost everything in our prodigality; but we rise again, thanks to God whose love endures even when we fail.

What sustained this young man even in his rebellion? The answer is simple. The love of God. The fallen must respond to God's love. For divine love demands our free and conscious response for it to become active in our lives. This does not mean that God stops loving us because we have not responded. No, the love of God is ever present, but we miss out on the fruits that this love seeks to bear in our lives if we fail to respond to it in kind. We must never forget that the transitional note is always a note of divine love. "For God commendeth his love toward us, in that, while we were yet sinners, Christ died for us" (Romans 5:8). It is this unconditional love that is a bridge from our dolefulness to a vivified consciousness. As the story progresses: Jesus lays out the steps. First there must be a raising of consciousness. This is the quickening of our being from false consciousness to facing the truth.

Chapter Three

VICTORY OVER GRIEF

BASED ON MARK 5:1-19, 21-24, 35-43

Mark 5:1-19

And they came over unto the other side of the sea, into the country of the Gadarenes. ²And when he was come out of the ship, immediately there met him out of the tombs a man with an unclean spirit, ³Who had his dwelling among the tombs; and no man could bind him, no, not with chains: ⁴Because that he had been often bound with fetters and chains, and the chains had been plucked asunder by him, and the fetters broken in pieces: neither could any man tame him. ⁵And always, night and day, he was in the mountains, and in the tombs, crying, and cutting himself with stones. ⁶But when he saw Jesus afar off, he ran and worshipped him, ⁷And cried with a loud voice, and said, What have I to do with thee, Jesus, thou Son of the most high God? I adjure thee by God, that thou torment me not. ⁸For he said unto him, Come out of the man, thou unclean spirit. ⁹And he asked him, What is thy name? And he answered, saying, My name is Legion: for we are many. ¹⁰And he besought him much that he would not send them away out of the country. ¹¹Now there was there nigh unto the mountains a great herd of swine feeding. ¹²And all the devils besought him, saying, Send us into the swine, that we may enter into them. ¹³And forthwith Jesus gave them leave. And the unclean spirits went out, and entered into the swine: and the herd ran violently down a steep place into the sea, (they were about two thousand;) and were choked in the sea. ¹⁴And they that fed the swine fled, and told it in the city, and in the country. And they went out to see what it was that was done. ¹⁵And they come to Jesus, and see him that was possessed with the devil, and had the legion, sitting, and clothed, and in his right mind: and they were afraid. ¹⁶And they that saw it told them how it befell to him that was possessed with the devil, and also concerning the swine. ¹⁷And they began to pray him to depart out of their coasts. ¹⁸And when he was come into the ship, he that had been possessed with the devil prayed him that he might be with him. *19Howbeit Jesus suffered him not, but saith unto him, Go home to thy friends, and tell them how great things the Lord hath done for thee, and hath had compassion on thee.*

Mark 5:21-24

And when Jesus was passed over again by ship unto the other side, much people gathered unto him: and he was nigh unto the sea. *22 And, behold, there cometh one of the rulers of the synagogue, Jairus by name; and when he saw him, he fell at his feet,* *23 And besought him greatly, saying, My little daughter lieth at the point of death: I pray thee, come and lay thy hands on her, that she may be healed; and she shall live.* *24 And Jesus went with him; and much people followed him, and thronged him.*

Mark 5:35-43

While he yet spake, there came from the ruler of the synagogue's house certain which said, Thy daughter is dead: why troublest thou the Master any further? *36 As soon as Jesus heard the word that was spoken, he saith unto the ruler of the synagogue, Be not afraid, only believe.* *37 And he suffered no man to follow him, save Peter, and James, and John the brother of James.* *38 And he cometh to the house of the ruler of the synagogue, and seeth the tumult, and them that wept and wailed greatly.* *39 And when he was come in, he saith unto them, Why make ye this ado, and weep? The damsel is not dead, but sleepeth.* *40 And they laughed him to scorn. But when he had put them all out, he taketh the father and the mother of the damsel, and them that were with him, and entereth in where the damsel was lying.* *41 And he took the damsel by the hand, and said unto her, Talitha cumi; which is, being interpreted, Damsel, I say unto thee, arise.* *42 And straightway the damsel arose, and walked; for she was of the age of twelve years. And they were astonished with great astonishment.* *43 And he charged them straitly that no man should know it; and commanded that something should be given her to eat.*

Growing up, I lost three siblings to childhood diseases. I still recall the grief of each death. Even today when I think about my baby brother, Paul, I feel a pang of that sadness. I recall the wailing of the women. I can still visualize the despondency in the face of the men. Because he was at the age of adolescence, his loss was especially painful. I remember that for months I was convinced that I saw my brother's face. It was especially acute when I walked through the burial ground to the farm. What has stuck with me to this day is the depth of the capacity to feel sorrow. But not only the capacity for feeling sorrow but the capacity for the expression of sorrow. Africans in the villages have a way of expressing grief that wrenches even the heart of the most stalwart. I watched as men who were of stone character melted in the wake of the expression of grief which attended the loss of a child or the loss of anyone.

As I grew and came to believe in the possibility of bodily resurrection, I realized that this sorrow was expressed not just for the young but for the elders also. The grief has not left completely, but my perspective on such grief that has been transformed by my deeper understanding of life, death and resurrection. But death, is not the only cause of the grief we know as human beings. As I write at the present moment, I grieve over my son who has been gifted with so many gifts, it seems that God has favored him beyond his contemporaries. Yet he cannot seem to find his bearing toward fruitfulness. Many who have spent sleepless nights praying their children through a maze of foolishness also understand this grief. I can see the grief upon their faces. They grieve. I grieve. But there is One to whom we must turn for a deeper connection. He is called a "man of sorrow acquainted with grief."

Though the sense of loss is more deeply felt at the death or absence of beloved ones, this is not the only loss which we encounter in our earthly journey. There are losses of small and great proportion. There are easily dismissible losses and losses which take with them a whole part of our humanity and create an uncoverable void. Within the Scriptures, we find all kinds of examples of losses. We find the loss of innocence never to be regained, not even in the kingdom of God. This innocence is replaced not with new innocence but with blamelessness.

The pain of loss is a general experience of human beings.

Loss changes our posture. It has a direct impact upon our lives. Loss unnerves us and frees us to become vulnerable. The uncovering we find in the loss that happened with our first parents, Adam and Eve, is ever present and needs the intervention of God to cover it again. Loss shows our tendency to cover ourselves; we limit exposure of our insecurities. Some of us are adept at hiding our feelings in the face of loss. In fact today, it is common to deny the pain of loss. Some even confuse this denial with faith while others call it positive thinking. We have to guard against the denial that masks as faith. For every lie is antithetical to faith. Thus the denial of loss is antithetical to faith.

One might point out in the text that when Jesus says "the child is not dead but sleepeth" it is denial of what is obviously real. That point is well taken. Statements of faith should never be discounted. Jesus' statement is not a denial based on unbelief, but a denial which is grounded in faith. The denial which leads to faith is usually followed with an affirmation. "The child is not dead" is denial—and it would be a lie if the child is truly dead—but Jesus adds "but sleepeth" which is an affirmation of faith. Faith language is not oversimplified, as some might label it. It is common in the Scripture.

One of the best examples of this denial and affirmation is David's statement "I shall not die" for as we know David did die. But David turns it into an affirmation when he adds "but I shall live to declare the works of God." To have victory over a loss, we do not need to deny the loss in such a way that it becomes a lie, but to deny it in such a way that it grows into an affirmation. When Jesus states "the child is not dead," He denies what everyone accepts as a matter of course. He denies that death as a principle of loss is the ultimate and final word. He denies it and inserts an affirmation. His affirmation redefines the situation so that it is seen in a new light. He changes the language and finality of death by affirming the possibility of recovery— "but sleepeth." As we all know, "sleep" is a euphemism for death. Thus, the finality of death is denied by the word of faith.

Victory over death and the grief it causes is sealed by an affirmation of faith. It is true that all human loss does not allow for such reinterpretation. It may not help you in your situation for me to tell you to deny the reality of what is happening to you. It is at times a difficult challenge to accept that reinterpreting your situation through the eyes of the Son of God will help you affirm the possibility of life and newness. How can denial and affirmation help? When a young person has lost his/her innocence through abuse, is there a word which can help to change the fact? There is no word which can remove the reality of the loss, but there is a word which denies finality of such abuse and affirms the possibility of new life in such a situation.

When one loses a loved one to the grim reaper, as we find here in this passage, words cannot remove the reality of that loss. But there is a word spoken by the Master which both denies the pretense of the finality of death and affirms the possibility of life after death. What does one do when marriage is broken and love once held dear is shattered? Is there a word that can change the fact that it happened? The answer may be no, but there is a word spoken by the Master which denies its power to end your life and affirms the possibility of a new beginning through forgiveness and divine comfort.

When one loses one's material fortune and is left destitute, or when an innocent man loses his freedom through a series of twisted injustices parading as justice, what word can one speak? It would be cruel in all of these cases to simply deny that what happened is real and painful. But in all of our losses the question must be asked, how can we begin anew? How can we rise from the burning ashes? How can we, whose heaviness has dragged us to the very lowest swim to the surface again? Is it possible to live again? To live anew? Is it possible to regain one's bearing? Is resurrection possible?

The answer must be a denial of the devil's lie. His rumor of our death must be denied; his reality must not become our reality. His geography must not be our dwelling place. The enemy's fiction must not become our fact. But we must not spend all our life denying what the enemies say—we must affirm what our reality must become in order for us to live and thrive. When Jesus says to the man "Be not afraid, only believe" (Mark 5:36), He was speaking directly of the fear of loss which takes hold of us and weakens us until we begin to confess what we ought to deny. In these two passages, we find two stories which go to the very heart of human loss and the desire to regain that which is lost.

Mark 5:1-19 is the story of one who lost everything. Jesus and His disciples had traveled to the east side of Lake Galilee to an area near Gergasa. Immediately upon His arrival, a man possessed with demons ran up to Jesus. The demons were called Legion (Mark 5:9) because there were so many of them. A Roman legion consisted of 6,000 foot-soldiers. We cannot be certain of the actual number of demons possessing the man. However, there were enough of them to keep the poor man homeless and wandering naked within the region. In fact, he lost the most precious commodity on which all other gains are grounded—his mind.

We say in playfulness, or sometimes anger, "Have you lost your mind?" But can we really understand the depth of what it means to lose one's mind? This man who has lost his mind, we do not even know his name, is seen simply as the demonic. How disturbing it would be to lose your mind—to stand in a place where you are conscious of yourself and yet not have that grasp of consciousness which makes you who you are.

What a great loss. This man had lost his mind—his very self—to others over whom he had no power. This was a fundamental loss of control. This inner loss led to outward losses of great proportion. He lost his mind, his friends, his family, and his religious consciousness. To many, such a loss was final. In fact, the depth of this loss is seen in the fact that he spent his time among the dead. He made his home in the grave. Life lost its appeal for this man. The text tells us that he was chained, but he broke the chains and escaped. Yet, he lacked the ability to break the inner chains.

We do not know what led this man to lose his mind. We know that he was possessed by demons. So we can indeed say that spiritual principles and powers contributed to his loss. The devil ganged up on him with hordes of destructive demons. There are those who seem to think that there is no such thing as demon possession. But if we take the Bible seriously, we must admit that it is full of the evidence of a power beyond us whose main work seems to be geared toward causing us to lose that which is valuable to us. This in no way excuses our own activities and weaknesses which may lay the foundation for our own loss. But there are incidents where even the strong among us must reckon with spiritual wickedness in high and low places.

So the question is, what led to this possession? How did this man come to be susceptible to these destructive spirits thus opening himself up to such loss? It will not do just to say the devil did it, though the devil's participation cannot be denied. Sometimes we open the door to our mind which then allows the enemy a spiritual foothold in the territory of our souls. There are several ways in which human beings lose their mind and open themselves up to the enemy. Sometimes our loss of mind or of our spiritual equilibrium derives from deliberate practice of bad habits. There are those who open themselves up by getting into illicit relationships. Others get into trouble by what they eat and some through what they drink. Others yet by what kinds of spirits they associate with. For this man the loss was so deep that he made his home among the dead.

If we do not find a way to redefine it and get power over it, loss can place us in a situation where we live among the dead. Think of how many people have walked into a bar and drank themselves to destruction because of a loss. Think of how many have taken illegal drugs or have been hooked on crack because they cannot deal with a profound loss that they have experienced. How many go from one bed to another as a means of attempting to regain what they have lost in earlier times?

Note that this man saw Jesus, then ran and fell at His feet. What I am about to say is not written explicitly in the text, but it would seem that the evil spirits were not the source of his humility. For it is never the intention of the enemy to place us in a position where we can come face to face with deliverance. The enemies that had brought so much loss to this man were afraid of being in the presence of the Lord. They knew that being in His presence meant that this man was now on his road to recovery. Something deep inside the man caused him to seek freedom from his loss, to regain himself, his family, and his friends and in fact his God consciousness. That something caused the man to run to Jesus, fall on his knees, and worship Him.

Jesus recognized the man's desperate situation and ordered the demons to come out of him. The demons begged Jesus to allow them to enter a nearby herd of swine. Jesus gave them permission, and the demons left the man and entered the swine. When the demons entered the swine, the pigs ran down the hill and drowned. Here we see the very nature of man as designed by God. Even loss of mind does not necessarily mean the loss of the divine homing beacon placed within our soul. No matter how much we have lost, no matter how far gone we seem, there is within each one of us a principle which recognizes God's presence and understands that there is in God's presence the possibility of regaining what was lost. There is within our God the hope that we can begin anew and redirect our lives.

The entrance of Jesus into his situation changes the course of the man's life. In fact when He enters, no matter how many demons have made their abode within our lives, no matter how powerful they may have been, no matter how long they have held what they stole from us, when Jesus comes in, the battle becomes redefined and our consciousness is raised. We see hope where there was no hope and we see gain where heretofore there was loss, only loss. Jesus is able to return to us that which the enemy has taken from us.

The enemy had taken such a hold on him that all he could do was fall down at the Master's feet. He had even lost his voice. All that was left was the voice of the tormenting spirits. They cared not for the man but for themselves. They pleaded not for him but for themselves. They had tormented him, taken everything from him, but in the presence of the Master the enemy must restore that which he has taken. They knew that it was time for them to payback in restitution what they had taken by force or by farce from this man. Jesus restored to this man his mind, his family, and his friends. He could not literally regain the years which the enemy had taken, but his life's direction was changed in such a way that from now on he had power over those who formerly had power over him. Now he had power to loose himself from those who had bound him. Jesus instructed him to go back home and tell what great things the Lord had done for him.

The story of this man and his deliverance establishes for us, beyond question, that the Lord descends into the very pit of our despair and into the blind alleys of our loss—even where it seems that it is impossible to articulate the pain of our souls. As the psalmist states, "Thou wilt not leave my soul in hell" (Psalm 16:10). So the Lord will not allow us to dwell in the despair of our loss. We must venture into His presence. With Him we must affirm the possibility of our revivification. As it is impossible for Jesus to be held captive by the pains of hell, or to be kept as a prisoner to eternal loss, so it becomes possible for us to gain release by His presence.

Have you experienced loss that has shaken you to your very core? Christ was in hell and came out alive. So will you. Are you in the graveyard enclosed by a giant boulder? Jesus was buried, enclosed, and tied down, yet He rose again from the grave. So can you by His power working in you. As we hang upon a cross not of our own making, what can we do? Remember that He hung on the cross and made a door to salvation.

If He broke off the chains by which He had been bound, which sought to steal freedom and even His life, can He not also release us from the possibility of eternal loss? If we have lost the knowledge of ourself, He is the teacher, the very heart of wisdom which restores self-knowledge. If we have lost friends, He is the One who is the very foundation of friendship; He will create for us the environment whereby we can again befriend both ourselves and others. To believe in Him is to prepare ourselves to lose those pains which grew out of the hold of what we have lost. He is able to resolve our conflict by granting us deliverance.

Some may think that believers are presumptuous in trying to redefine situations of loss through Jesus Christ. In fact, some theologians call this a psychological defense mechanism—denial. But how can we read this man's story and not be led to believe in the possibility of healing and divine restoration of that which the cankerworm has eaten? For you see all those who find Him, or rather are found by Him, were delivered from the state of loss and promised a new beginning.

There are many of us who were lost but are now found. There are several who have lost much but through His power have regained all. All who come to Him are delivered without exception. This victory comes not from some magical power but from One who knows the depth of human pain. He gives victory over loss. Who will not rejoice when their lost mind has been restored? Who will not rejoice to receive victory over loss and now stand to regain through the power of the Lord? Imagine what joy, especially for the man who had so intimately known the loss of himself, now sitting and having power over his thoughts and imagination. What victory for the man who lost even the ability to speak for himself, whose eloquence and talent was submerged by demonic powers, to be able to join the poets and orators of God's Word. For Jesus says to him, "go tell all the good things which the Lord has done for you."

Jesus Christ the Saviour delivers all from that place of loss and despair. In fact, He has come to empty the halls of hell. From the time of His appearance to this day, and even unto the end of the world, He is in the work of restoring that which we have lost. He has spoken victory and the power of loss resulting in meaninglessness is made ineffectual and the pains of hell's thievery are removed by His word.

But the loss experienced in the life of the Gaderene demoniac is not the only loss which Jesus healed in this chapter. Many have looked at the death of the daughter of Jairus, the ruler of the synagogue, from the perspective of the child and that of the mourners. But we need to look at it from the perspective of a parent who has lost a child. What a great loss! Can

Jesus do anything about such great loss? What can God know about such loss that is not theoretical divine knowledge? It is at the presence of death that we human beings feel the finality of loss.

The story at the beginning of this chapter in which I describe the feelings which I had at the loss of my siblings is true. I had a sense of finality that no words can explain. As a child I walked around wondering if this is what life is all about. You live, you die. Is that the end? But more than that, for my parents there was no explanation for the death of this child. I can still feel the frustration of my mother, her deep sigh, my father's silent tears and deep sobs and sometimes the questions whispered through his beard—"why my child?" Through all of this, there was hope that this was not the end.

The wailing female relative caused deep anxiety that was noticeable in the faces of the children who knew something was wrong but did not understand what it was. It was this fear of loss which led the father to the request in Mark 5:22-23. After the Jews were taken into Babylonian captivity, the synagogue became the designated place of worship. Services in the synagogue followed the same pattern as those held at the temple in Jerusalem, except there were no animal sacrifices. According to Jewish Law animal sacrifices could only be offered in the temple at Jerusalem.

Is a loss felt more because one is a ruler of the synagogue, with responsibilities that include maintaining the facilities and assigning people to carry out the worship services? Is there a greater sense of loss for one who is responsible for discipline as opposed to those who are disciplined? (John 9:22, 16:2) Is loss greater for the administrator than it is for the staff? Is loss greater for the scourger than it is for the scourged? (Matthew 10:17; Mark 13:9) Is loss greater for the rulers of the synagogue who were usually men of great wealth than it is for the poor? The answer is no. A wise man named Qoheleth once answered: "As it happens to the poor so it does for the rich." At such times, we must look beyond our material status to overcome what is common to all us.

Since rulers of the synagogue were men of vast riches, it may be assumed, safely, that Jairus had spent a significant portion of his wealth trying to help his daughter. Jairus' position as synagogue ruler and his wealth had proven useless in saving his daughter. The young girl was now at the point of death. In desperation, Jairus decided to turn to Jesus for help. This step was either one of courage or desperation. For you see, many Jews followed Jesus, but many others, especially the Jewish religious leaders, were greatly offended by some of His teachings. In spite of the controversy surrounding Jesus, Jairus was willing to risk his position and reputation to save his beloved daughter.

Jesus and His disciples had crossed the Sea of Galilee, landing at Capernaum. As soon as Jesus left the boat, a huge crowd gathered around Him. Jairus made his way through the crowd and fell at Jesus' feet. Although Jairus was a civic and religious leader in Capernaum, he addressed Jesus with humility and reverence. "My little daughter is dying. Please come and put your hands on her so that she will be healed and live" (Mark 5:23, NIV). He has come to the understanding which the wise ancients had learned: position, power, riches, and prestige cannot ease the despair which can torment the human soul.

Loss has a way of forcing us to find our way to God. Jairus had to turn in trust to Jesus for help. In times of grief and loss, many of us become vulnerable to trusting shifting sands around us. But we must take heed and listen to the Scripture's command that our trust must be placed right where our victory is to be realized. When our loss is great, we need to resolve like Job in chapter 13:15: "Though He slay me, yet will I trust Him." At such times, we must resolve to trust God. By placing his trust in Jesus at the time of his great loss, Jairus joined the select number whom the psalmist proclaims in the divine benediction in Psalm 2:12—"Blessed are all those who put their trust in Him."

Offerings are no good unless accompanied with trust. There are those who attempt to overcome their despair by doing a good deed here and there, but for true renewal, acts must be accompanied with trust. Psalm 4:5 says, "Offer the sacrifices of righteousness, And put your trust in the Lord."

Such trust is what leads to our preservation even in the face of the enemy's onslaught (Psalm 16:1). And to gain victory, we must not misplace our trust. There were some in Jairus' midst who trusted their own knowledge or other powers. Even David acknowledged that "Some trust in chariots, and some in horses" (Psalm 20:7a). There may be those around you who seem to prosper because they put themselves first. They trust in material things and false gods. But you and I must in the midst of our loss remember to say, "let them do what they will, but we will remember the name of the Lord our God" (Psalm 20:7b, paraphrased). Loss sometimes results in shame, but trusting the Lord safeguards us from the destructive nature of shame. I hear the psalmist say in Psalm 25:2:

O my God, I trust in You;
Let me not be ashamed;
Let not my enemies triumph over me.

Not only does trust in God safeguard us from the destructive shame which so often accompanies loss, but trust in God defeats the enemy. What does the enemy want in both texts? For the demoniac to hide himself for shame in the graveyard and for Jairus to cover his face in shame from a society which wrongly believes that tragedies only befall sinners.

Though the text does not say it, we know that because he was a ruler of the synagogue, the death of his daughter would have raised questions about his righteousness. There would have been shame hanging over him. In fact, those who did not like him may have used it as an opportunity to try to depose him from his position. But through trust in Jesus, his shame was washed away and whatever enemy may have risen against him was neutralized before it could start. The only way to truly neutralize shame and the enemy is to trust. Though our friends may be reluctant to trust the Lord, we must say with David in Psalm 31:14-15.

But as for me, I trust in You, O LORD;
I say, "You are my God."

It is through trust that this man was able to experience the faithfulness of the Lord. Whatever you and I do in the time of our trouble, may we say like David that we "will not trust in my bow," because we know that our own weapons will not save us (Psalm 44:6). The trust of Jairus brought Jesus to his doorstep and into his house and to the bedchamber where He healed Jairus' daughter, and thereby healed his shame and fear.

The laying on of hands was done to communicate authority, power, or blessing (see Genesis 48:18) and is often seen in connection with healing (Matthew 9:18; Acts 28:8). Jesus agreed to answer the man's desperate plea, and they started for Jairus' house. When we grieve, the crowd that surrounds us can serve to highlight our momentary existential isolation. It is not that others do not empathize or understand the grief we now feel, rather it is because in such instances we stand in need not of human sympathy but of divine empathy. Only God, at such moments, can reach us at the depth of our psychic disequilibrium.

As a ruler of the synagogue, Jairus was aware of the regulations concerning ceremonial cleanliness. If Jesus were touched by an unclean person such as the bleeding woman, then He too would be considered unclean. This meant that Jesus would then be forbidden to touch anyone for 24 hours. Jairus had told Jesus that his daughter was near death and required His immediate attention. Now Jesus had publicly acknowledged that He had been touched by an unclean woman, and that He had healed her. Things seemed to be going from bad to worse for poor Jairus. But he held his tongue and placed his trust in Jesus rather than ceremony.

POWER OF JESUS: VICTORY OVER SIN AND SICKNESS

BASED ON MARK 2:3-12

Mark 2:3-12

And they come unto him, bringing one sick of the palsy, which was borne of four. ⁴And when they could not come nigh unto him for the press, they uncovered the roof where he was: and when they had broken it up, they let down the bed wherein the sick of the palsy lay. ⁵When Jesus saw their faith, he said unto the sick of the palsy, Son, thy sins be forgiven thee. ⁶But there were certain of the scribes sitting there, and reasoning in their hearts, ⁷Why doth this man thus speak blasphemies? who can forgive sins but God only? ⁸And immediately when Jesus perceived in his spirit that they so reasoned within themselves, he said unto them, Why reason ye these things in your hearts? ⁹Whether is it easier to say to the sick of the palsy, Thy sins be forgiven thee; or to say, Arise, and take up thy bed, and walk? ¹⁰But that ye may know that the Son of man hath power on earth to forgive sins, (he saith to the sick of the palsy,) ¹¹I say unto thee, Arise, and take up thy bed, and go thy way into thine house. ¹²And immediately he arose, took up the bed, and went forth before them all; insomuch that they were all amazed, and glorified God, saying, We never saw it on this fashion.

The key to this entire passage of Scripture is found in the words spoken by the Master to the skeptics and religious doubters at the healing of the paralytic: "But that ye may know that the Son of man hath power on earth to forgive sins, (he saith to the sick of the palsy,) I say unto thee, Arise, and take up thy bed, and go thy way into thine house" (Mark 2:10-11). It seems that healing, especially when it is tied to faith, is always a controversial issue. Controversy especially as related to the source of Jesus' power or even His authority to do the things which He did is the key element in the five incidents that Mark describes in this section (Mark 2:1-3:5). In each incident, Jesus is either covertly (2:6-7; 3:2) or overtly (2:16, 18, 24) challenged by the religious leaders, but also implied is the challenge to His authority and power. The use of His power offended some. The affirmation of His power over what human beings see as impossible led to questions such as "Why doth this man thus speak blasphemies?" (2:7) If His words offended, so did His actions: "How is it that he eateth and drinketh with publicans and sinners?" (v. 16)

The use of His power gave people victory over oppressive traditions and offended the keepers of tradition: "Why do the disciples of John and of the Pharisees fast, but thy disciples fast not?" (v. 18, see also v. 24). You see, true victory leads to freedom, and Jesus affirmed His power so that those who came into contact with Him could gain power and then become free from all situations of oppression that may have plagued them.

It is unlikely that the five events in this section happened in the order that Mark presents them. The writer probably lumps the incidents together because of their common element of conflict between Jesus and the religious leaders. Taken together, the incidents validate Jesus' authority over sickness, death, the Law, and religious traditions. In today's study, we will examine the first and last conflicts relating the authority and power of Jesus as the Messiah. Here we also see some things over which we can be victorious because Jesus the Son of the Living God is with us.

Jesus gives us victory over sin and over the effects of sin (Mark 2:1-12). Near the end of Jesus' preaching campaign in Galilee, the crowds became so large that Jesus could not openly preach in the cities and towns. He withdrew to solitary places, but even there the people followed Him (Mark 1:45). After completing the Galilean campaign, Jesus returned to His home base in Capernaum. Word of His return spread throughout the city with amazing speed, and soon the crowds began to gather again. Even when Jesus retired to the home where He

was staying, the multitude followed Him. The immense crowd filled the house and spilled out into the street, making it impossible to reach the door from the street. In spite of all the uninvited guests, Jesus did what came naturally to Him—"He preached the word unto them" (2:2).

In the house that day were many Pharisees who had traveled from all over Israel to investigate Jesus' ministry. The Pharisees had every right to investigate the new rabbi because they were responsible for supervising the nation's religious life (Deuteronomy 13). There was a man in the city who had missed Jesus' sunset healing service (Mark 1:32-34). When the news of Jesus' return reached him, he saw a chance for healing of his paralysis. But he needed help to get to Jesus. Fortunately, the stricken man knew four people who cared enough about him to help him. Each man grabbed a corner of the padded quilt the man was lying on and used it as a stretcher to carry him. When the group arrived at the house, they found that carrying the load was only the beginning of their problem. "They could not get him to Jesus because of the crowd" (2:4a).

The four men were deeply concerned for their friend, and they believed that Jesus could and would heal him. Instead of becoming discouraged at the difficulty of their task, they decided to find a way to overcome the problem. After trying and failing to push their way through the crowd, the group went around to the side of the house. There they found a stairway and carefully carried the stretcher up the stairs to the roof.

The roofs of homes in ancient Israel were usually made of branches, straw, and mud. Although sturdy enough to walk on, the roofs were easily torn apart, and that is exactly what our determined group did. "They uncovered the roof where he was: and when they had broken it up, they let down the bed wherein the sick of the palsy lay" (v. 4b). It would have been easy for the men to give up after traveling to the house only to find their way blocked when they arrived. But their compassion for their stricken comrade and their belief in Jesus motivated them to persevere. Their compassion and conviction would soon be rewarded by a word of victory over sin and sickness.

We have victory over sin because Jesus clearly expressed power over sin. We have this power not because we are able to live a sinless life but because Jesus speaks forgiveness into our situation. Jesus was in the house preaching when He was suddenly interrupted by a strange sight. A man lying on a mattress was being lowered from the roof to the floor by four other men. Jesus recognized their bold maneuver as an act of love and faith. He responded to their courageous effort with a totally unexpected statement: "Son, thy sins be forgiven thee" (v. 5). The religious leaders were stunned! Only God could forgive sin (Isaiah 43:25). Jesus was laying claim to something that only God could do. The Pharisees were sure they had what they had come for—Jesus was guilty of blasphemy! Or was he?

The religious leaders did not say anything, but Jesus looked into their hearts and saw their critical spirits. He knew they were accusing Him of blasphemy (see John 2:25). The scribes and Pharisees were correct; Jesus was claiming divine authority for Himself. However, their assessment of the situation was wrong because Jesus, the Messiah, has every right to forgive sin. While God has given several wonderful gifts to us sinners, all His gifts are grounded in the person of Jesus. And one of the major gifts is that of forgiveness. Some might think that it does not take much to forgive sins. But from the perspective of the religious leaders present at the healing of the paralytic it does take formidable power to forgive sins.

Sin is ingrained in the very soul of human beings because human beings are by nature sinful; we can say that sin is interwoven in the very fabric of our lives. It will take more than words to release us from this serpent coiled around the human heart. This was what God had been working on for the millennia—to finally say to humanity, "your sins are forgiven."

How is one to receive victory over sins when one is caught in an abnormal situation? First, one must reach beyond oneself. Second, one must hear a voice other than that which has been ringing in one's head. In this case, one must hear the voice of Jesus. Our lives are characterized by the phenomena of noise pollution—the voices from places and people who do not have our healthful interest at heart. These voices can seek to define us and socialize us in particular ways. Some seek to convince us that our happiness depends on the condition created by this phenomena of unintegrated noise.

The voice which this man needed to hear was a voice which was distinct from the voices which he was accustomed to hearing. Why does this man need to disregard the voices in his head and those of society? Simply, those voices represent the condition from which he needs deliverance. They reinforce his pain. These voices affirm his self pity, hopelessness, and despair. When one has been sick for so long from paralysis of the mind, there is no healing and wholeness outside of relationship with God.

The presence of sickness continuously reminds us that we are broken spiritually as well as physically. Sin eliminates our desire to put in place our own solution to our problems with God. It would take more than all the powers of the world to release humanity from the shackles of this thing called sin. It would take more than all the waters of the world to wash humanity from this stain. How dare this man speak these words with such ease?

Jesus' words of forgiveness raise the issue of power and the Pharisees' statement "only God" gets to the heart of the matter. "Only God" has the capacity to forgive sins. Yet Jesus was laying claim to the very nature of God. He used no formula invoking someone else's name, rather He spoke with direct authority. It is sin that keeps us from entering into the fullness of what God has for us. God gave the Son to make this power manifest. In fact, it is because He has this power that sin's power can be broken. If you have Jesus, the power of sin is broken.

Note that I did not say that you will never sin. But I said that its power is broken. The wages of sin is death, but even death has been conquered. The grave has no more authority, its bargaining power has been taken away. But many will misunderstand. How can something which has held humanity for so long be broken by a simple spoken word? Forgiveness can happen without healing but healing, if it is true, cannot be complete without forgiveness; it cannot be accomplished without the grace attending forgiveness.

The ancients tied forgiveness to the removal of acts resulting in a covenantal breach. Before true healing could occur, in their opinion, this breach of covenant had to be healed. Some say that forgiveness cannot precede faith. That may be so, but in this text the man does not seem to ask for it. If that is the case then faith in their context is derived from his friends. Sometimes the first step to our victory must be taken for us by another. Sometimes the seed of our faith is lent to us by another. Jesus saw the faith of his friends and honored that faith. Whether faith must precede forgiveness or not, as some theologians argue, we may never know, but what we know is that forgiveness denotes the end of the old and the beginning of the new. Forgiveness expresses the new as depending on the activity and nature of the Messiah. There is nothing in the text that tells us that the paralytic was conscious of his sin, but Jesus highlights the presence of his sin as a hindrance to his wholeness. Jesus is not the only one who does this. David does the same in Psalm:103:3, so does James in 5:16.

Forgiveness is not about perfection. In fact it reminds us of our humanity. I wonder if the anger of the Pharisees was because Jesus' words "your sins are forgiven" reminded them of their own unresolved sins. Did His words remind them of the weight under which they labored? Forgiveness will not remove life's ups and downs or keep you from ever falling, but it gives you the power to start anew within yourself and so gain the courage to start anew with others and let them also start anew.

Those who have not been forgiven have not yet experienced the joy of self-consciousness infused by the divine. Those who have not felt the power of divine forgiveness leading them to an energized self-discovery have difficulty letting others discover themselves. You see, while forgiveness helps us to begin anew, it has to first remind us that we are fallen. But once one hears Jesus say, "your sins are forgiven," psychic terrain expands and love lights anew upon the restless soul. Forgiveness coming from Christ is a spiritual transcendence moving one into the heart of God.

Forgiveness transforms our desires. This man in this passage and his friends may have thought that he was only in need of physical healing. However the search of human beings is a fundamental search for inner peace resulting in joy. Not even his physical healing would have delivered this man. Physical healing may be solely the reconstitution of the finite which still leaves our yearning for the infinite unsatisfied. The paralytic's need for physical healing also was linked to something beyond the physical. Human beings are spiritual beings whose fundamental needs cannot be satisfied by the ways of the world. How many times have we tried to solve our spiritual problems with mere material covering? Sometimes even in our well-intentioned actions we find that we have missed the inner meaning of the event in which we are engaged. None who surrounded this man seemed to have understood the depth of his need. Maybe even he himself did not grasp the depth of his need. But this is not just the problem of the physically sick.

How many times in the church do we confuse spiritual needs with physical necessity. We reorganize when what is needed is repentance; we start a building program when what we need is to clean the spiritual house; we engage in bureaucratic gymnastics and politicizing when what we need is prayer. The church is a spiritual entity whose physical ailment must first be approached in terms of the dynamic of her spiritual life. Forgiveness must precede organizational formulas.

How many times has our church sought healing without forgiveness? How often do we want the symptoms to disappear without dealing with the core problem? Jesus, ignoring the convention of healers who concentrated on the physical ailment, went to a deeper place and there He spoke a word from which true healing emerged: "your sins are forgiven." The man sick of the palsy was forgiven in public, in the sight of the people. It is in the forgiveness which we receive from the Lord that the glory and excellence of our God shines forth.

Forgiveness makes the weak strong and causes the fallen to stand. Sin creates fear but the forgiveness which one receives from Jesus renews us limb by limb and restores our spiritual energies. Forgiveness that comes from the Christ infuses within us moral courage removing timidity. The Pharisees were right in asking their question, "Who can forgive sins, but God alone?" for in their midst stood One who "was manifested to take away our sins; and in him is no sin" (1 John 3:5). Here the promise of the Lord God to us is that which says "Though your sins be as scarlet, they shall be as radiant as falling snow; though they be red and congealed like crimson, they shall be like wool"(Isaiah 1:18, paraphrased).

Through Jesus, the Ninevites obtained forgiveness of their sins; He was the message of Nathan to David, "The Lord also hath put away thy sin, and thou shalt not die;" (2 Samuel 12:13). He is the forgiver of the guilt of Ahab and the pardoner of his blood-guiltiness. He is the forgiver of Israel in the wilderness. He is the Lord of frequent restoration. He is the One who said "I will have mercy not sacrifice" (Matthew 9:13). By forgiving this man his sin, Jesus put Himself in the center of divine power and renewal.

We read that "immediately when Jesus perceived in his spirit that they so reasoned within themselves, he said unto them, Why reason ye these things in your hearts?" (Mark 2:8) Then He challenged them with a counter-question: "Which is easier: to say to the paralytic, 'Your sins are forgiven,' or to say, 'Get up, take your mat and walk'?" (v. 9, NIV). The obvious answer is that it is much easier to say your sins are forgiven because no one can prove or disprove the person's forgiveness.

The religious leaders declined to answer His question, so Jesus continued. "But that you may know that the Son of Man has authority on earth to forgive sins . . . ." He said to the paralytic, "I tell you, get up, take your mat and go home" (vv. 10-11, NIV). This is the first time in Mark that Jesus refers to Himself as the Son of Man. The Jews knew this title applied to the Messiah (Daniel 7:13-14). Jesus was staking His claim to divinity.

The paralyzed man got up, picked up his mat, and walked out before the amazed eyes of Jesus' critics. The fact that the man was healed was proof that his sins were forgiven. The dazed Pharisees could not challenge Jesus' claim to the title "Son of Man," nor could they accuse Him of blasphemy. The faith of the paralyzed man and his four friends resulted in a threefold victory: The paralytic was healed, Jesus was vindicated, and God was glorified. Obstacles and opposition in our lives are opportunities for Christ to demonstrate His power in our behalf.

The controversy involving the man with the withered hand is the fifth conflict between Jesus and Israel's religious leaders. The religious leaders should have recognized the Messiah. Instead they saw Jesus as a threat to their status and power and chose to oppose Him. As was His custom, Jesus was in the synagogue on the Sabbath. In the service that morning was a man with a serious, though not life-threatening, affliction. The nerves and muscles of one of his hands had dried up, rendering the hand paralyzed. Also present that day were certain Pharisees who had come to see if Jesus would heal the man on the Sabbath Day.

The Pharisees were convinced that Jesus was a Sabbath violator. Like most aspects of Jewish life, the practice of medicine was strictly regulated by legal tradition. Giving medical attention on the Sabbath was only permitted if there was a chance the afflicted person might die without care. This was not the case for the man with the withered hand. And the Pharisees were watching closely to see if Jesus would heal the man. This was their chance to get rid of Him because Jewish law called for the execution of Sabbath violators (Exodus 35:2).

Jesus knew the Pharisees were trying to trap Him. He could have waited until after the service and healed the man privately, or He could have waited until the next day. Instead, Jesus made the healing as public as possible. He commanded the man to "Stand up in front of everyone" (Mark 3:3, NIV). All eyes in the synagogue watched to see what Jesus would do. Turning His attention to the Pharisees, Jesus asked, "Is it lawful to do good on the Sabbath days, or to do evil? to save life, or to kill?" (v. 4)

The Lord knew what the Pharisees had up their sleeves. He wanted to do good on the Sabbath, while they were planning evil. He wanted to give life to a dead hand, while they were looking for an excuse to take His life (v. 6). Again, Jesus had trapped the Pharisees with a question that had only one obvious answer. Realizing their predicament, the Pharisees swallowed their anger and held their tongues.

Now it was Jesus' turn to become angry. The Pharisees were more concerned with legal detail than with mercy and grace. They would rather see their precious traditions protected than to see the poor man healed. Turning back to the man, Jesus commanded him, "stretch forth thine hand" (v. 5). The man could have easily replied, "My hand is paralyzed, I can't move it." Instead, he obediently willed his useless hand to move. As he did so, the nerves in his hand suddenly sprang to life, sending impulses to the atrophied muscles. Then blood started flowing through the muscles allowing them to respond to the nerve impulses. The hand stretched out completely restored! The healing of the paralyzed man and the man with the withered hand affirmed Jesus' authority over sin, sickness, and human traditions. Jesus is not only the Lamb of God, He is the King of kings.

The need for a network of faith is vital for the healing of even those who suppose that they have strong faith. This man's healing was not a result of his individual ability. He had none. He needed others to help him get to the place of his healing. There is a characteristic of the modern society which is being co-opted by so many believers. This idea is in direct contrast to the biblical injunction to love one's neighbor. The world in its extreme secularity argues for individuals to watch out for number one. In fact those who cannot do for themselves are usually dismissed as being lazy.

Our society is fast becoming a society where those who have attained a certain degree of success forget about those who are still in the throes of death. The healthy put away the sick and forget about them. At other times our society's involvement is that of over-analyzing. We ask, how did she get this way? He must have been fooling around to get this way. Scholars spend inordinate amounts of time analyzing the social, historical causes of society's ills while never coming to aid the suffering. His friends did not sit around and ask philosophical questions regarding the cause of his sickness.

Notice also that they did not sit around and argue about Jesus, His nature, His power, or His upbringing. That was left to Pharisees and Sadducees. Neither do we find these brothers arguing about who will be in the front, or who will carry the rear of the bed. How often we spend so much time arguing over trifles while those who are sick get sicker and those who are hurting bleed to death. This man could not do for himself. He did not need the community arguing over his plight. He did not need his friends worried over who was going to get the credit for his healing.

It is amazing that we do not even know who came up with the idea to take him to Jesus. They just knew that it was time to do something. There are some folks who are never going to get well, get saved, or receive recovery unless we come together. It took the coming together of members of the community to initiate the healing process for this man. If we are interested in the birth of a future which preserves human dignity and hope, we cannot sit back and watch those who suffer. Notice also that the brothers did not just sit back and sympathize with this sick man. They got actively involved.

Jesus strongly encouraged a network of faith. His statement "where two or three are gathered there I am in their midst" (Matthew 18:20) is meant to discourage that faith which trumpets itself in aloneness and ignores the interconnected nature of spirituality. Just in case we think that only the sick need this helping hand, let us recall Moses.

There has never been a man more gifted in faith than Moses, yet at one point in his prayer life he needed members of the community to hold his hands up while he prayed. What we find here is not a network of spoken faith which says I believe that you can be healed but takes no physical step to assure healing. They believed and they acted. This network of faith is grounded in love. One cannot help but wonder how much these men loved their friend. It is a network of faith manifesting itself in love that will lead our world to the place of healing.

In John 15:12-14 Jesus said, "This is My commandment, that you love one another as I have loved you." He meant for us to build a web of love which reigns in all of God's children. For those who will ask what this means, Jesus proceeds further to state "Greater love has no one than this, than to lay down one's life for his friends." These men exemplified a network of faith webbed together by love. It was the faith of these four men that

Jesus saw and it parallels the fact that He Himself has broken the veil of heaven to carry us with all our paralysis into the presence of the Father.

We in the body of Christ are called to "love one another" as Jesus has loved us. It is through this act of faith and love that many passersby came to know the extent of the friendship of these four men for their paralyzed friend. We in the church have got quite a lot to learn from these men. Paul tells us in Romans 12:4-5 that "we, being many, are one body in Christ, and individually members of one another." If in fact this is the case, then those of us who are weak ought to count on the strong to be present in faith and love for us. Then those who are living spiritually ought to be there for those who are struggling with their spiritual life without judgment and resentment. This divine presence of the believer is the only debt we owe one another (Romans 13:8). But rather than carry each other and build each other up, many of us seem to be in the business of beating down the downtrodden, passing by the dying, and shunning the struggling. In fact, we seem to seek division and schism as a spiritual matter of fact. We take individualism to its demonic illogical conclusion.

But the men in this passage seem to understand intuitively what we Christians should see clearly according to 1 Corinthians 12:25-27, "that there should be no schism in the body, but that the members should have the same care for one another. And if one member suffers, all the members suffer with it; or if one member is honored, all the members rejoice with it. Now you are the body of Christ, and members individually." If in fact the body of Christ is a network of faith we ought to be servers where others who are needy can connect and find help. This is what we read "through love serve one another" in Galatians 5:13.

We must also become a serving station for one another that does not carry the virus of resentment, anger, or jealousy. Many of us serve, but when the served become strong we respond with resentment. From what we read here, these men were not among those who resented the healing of this man. How many times do churches reach out to heal a sinner and then resent the converted for being active? How many times do we heal and then resent the healed for being healed?

Our outreach in faith ought then to be carried out in the obedience to Ephesians 4:32, "And be kind to one another, tenderhearted, forgiving one another, just as God in Christ forgave you." The same compassion that leads us to reach out must lead us to reach in when those whom we have helped fail. In fact 1 Peter 3:8 hits it clearly by saying, "Finally, all of you be of one mind, having compassion for one another; love as brothers, be tenderhearted, be courteous." Apart from Moses on the mountain of prayer, the Hebrew Testament has another passage that brings this point home. In 2 Samuel 10:9-11 we read:

"When Joab saw that the battle line was against him before and behind, he chose some of Israel's best and put them in battle array against the Syrians. And the rest of the people he put under the command of Abishai his brother, that he might set them in battle array against the people of Ammon. Then he said, If the Syrians are too strong for me, then you shall help me; but if the people of Ammon are too strong for you, then I will come and help you."

Here we see at work the mutual dependence of faith which brings victory. As strong and experienced a soldier as Joab was he knew that he needed a network of faith to help him, so he surrounded himself with faithful soldiers who would come to his aid in his time of need. In the body of Christ, there is no need for any one to suffer alone. Are there any within the church who form a network of faith to serve the weak, to raise the downtrodden, and empower the powerless? This is the pathway to victory. This is the way to overcome the sickness that has so paralyzed our community. The people of God must build a network of faith webbed by love with each believer being a serving point to bring our community back to the Lord. So help us Lord.

STEPS ON THE WAY TO VICTORY

BASED ON JOSHUA 2:1, 8-14, 22-24

Joshua 2:1

And Joshua the son of Nun sent out of Shittim two men to spy secretly, saying, Go view the land, even Jericho. And they went, and came into an harlot's house, named Rahab, and lodged there.

Joshua 2:8-14

And before they were laid down, she came up unto them upon the roof; [9] *And she said unto the men, I know that the Lord hath given you the land, and that your terror is fallen upon us, and that all the inhabitants of the land faint because of you.* [10] *For we have heard how the Lord dried up the water of the Red sea for you, when ye came out of Egypt; and what ye did unto the two kings of the Amorites, that were on the other side Jordan, Sihon and Og, whom ye utterly destroyed.* [11] *And as soon as we had heard these things, our hearts did melt, neither did there remain any more courage in any man, because of you: for the Lord your God, he is God in heaven above, and in earth beneath.* [12] *Now therefore, I pray you, swear unto me by the Lord, since I have shown you kindness, that ye will also show kindness unto my father's house, and give me a true token:* [13] *And that ye will save alive my father, and my mother, and my brethren, and my sisters, and all that they have, and deliver our lives from death.* [14] *And the men answered her, Our life for yours, if ye utter not this our business. And it shall be, when the Lord hath given us the land, that we will deal kindly and truly with thee.*

Joshua 2:22-24

And they went, and came unto the mountain, and abode there three days, until the pursuers were returned: and the pursuers sought them throughout all the way, but found them not. [23] *So the two men returned, and descended from the mountain, and passed over, and came to Joshua the son of Nun, and told him all things that befell them:* [24] *And they said unto Joshua, Truly the Lord hath delivered into our hands all the land; for even all the inhabitants of the country do faint because of us.*

Around 2000 B.C. Abraham, the spiritual and natural father of the Jews was called by the Lord (Yahweh) God of Creation to leave the idolatry of his father Terah's household and go into the land of Canaan (Genesis 12:1-9; 13:15-18). The Lord told Abraham that his descendants would be slaves for 400 years, but after that they would be given the land that was promised to him and his descendants (Genesis 15:12-21). God promised Abraham that his descendants would be a great nation and that the whole earth would be blessed by them (Genesis 12:1-5; 15:1-6).

Soon after the time of Joseph, the Children of Israel were made slaves by the Egyptians (Exodus 1:7-14). After 400 years of this enslavement, Moses was called by God to deliver the Children of Israel from the oppression of the Egyptians through the miraculous parting of the Red Sea. God's act in saving Israel was meant to change Israel physically from people in chains to a free people. It was also meant to change their mindset from victims to victors. At every turn God performed miracles to help them change their perception of themselves. They were to be people walking in external and internal freedom. But instead of seizing this freedom they balked, they retreated and doubted. Thus, a journey that would have taken less than four months on foot took 40 years wandering around "in circles."

Now Moses, who brought them out to the borders of Canaan, was dead. Their parents were dead and there has been enough time for them to consider the actions of the former generation. The new leader is Joshua. Even his name embodied God's purpose—Joshua "the Lord is salvation" or "Yahweh (Jehovah) saves." Every time the Children of Israel said his name they were making a statement of faith about God's ability to save in all circumstances. Look at the genius of God. Who better to take over from Moses than one who went through the great events of the Passover and the Exodus with Moses?

Joshua's experience made him the logical leader of the people. At Sinai, Moses chose Joshua to assist him when he went onto the mountain to talk with God (Exodus 24:13). Moses also gave Joshua a prominent place in the service of the tabernacle. When Moses sent spies to scout the land of Canaan, only Joshua and Caleb returned to camp with a report that they could conquer the land with God's help. Because of their show of faith, only Joshua and Caleb were allowed to enter the land at the end of the Israelites' 40 years of wilderness wanderings. Joshua was also God's choice. God promised Joshua victory as he led the Children of Israel into the Promised Land of Canaan (Joshua 1:1-11).

What can we learn from this passage in Joshua in our walk to victory? Joshua 2:1 begins with Joshua sending out two spies secretly. The Hebrew words in this passage describe foot soldiers who were chosen by Joshua without the knowledge of the rest of the Israelites. This reconnaissance mission is very different from the public scouting assignment that Moses, by the direction of God, gave to Israel after they were freed from the oppression of the Egyptians. That public sending out of spies brought back a very negative report from most of the spies and resulted in Israel wasting 40 years in the wilderness.

Joshua probably chose his best foot soldiers because they had to swim the overflowing Jordan River, which only the best of swimmers could do, and they had to scout the land of Canaan, "especially Jericho" (2:1, NIV). Jericho is one of the oldest known, continually occupied cities in human history. Its origin goes back to at least 7000 B.C. These scouts also had to be good runners and mountain climbers and needed good eyesight and intelligence. They had to be in the best physical shape, and they had to be spiritually strong as well.

Here we learn the need to prepare for victory. As we seek to gain our victory we must not neglect the necessary preparation. Even those who serve the Lord must not neglect the physical, mental, and spiritual preparation required for living a victorious life. We will face spiritual as well as physical and mental challenges. We need to be as strong as possible to overcome the difficulties of life.

The camp of Israel was on the east side of the Jordan River in a place called *Shittim* which means the "place of Acacia tree groves." From the camp, the spies entered Jericho and slipped into the house of a prostitute named Rahab; the home was built into the city walls. In verses 2 through 7, the King of Jericho gets word of the coming of the spies and sends men to Rahab's house to capture them. She denies that they are there and sends the king's men on a "wild goose chase" up the road that leads to the Jordan River. But all the while, she had hidden the spies on the roof of her house. She placed herself in extreme danger in supporting the spies of Israel.

Rahab's unexpected and unsolicited confession in verses 8-11 is the core of this passage. Keep in mind that this nation, culture, and religion is an idolatrous one that does not respect the God of Israel. They worshiped the gods of the Canaanites, chiefly Baal. Rahab gives them six points that will encourage even the basest of cowards: (1) "I know that the Lord . . ."; (2) the land is already yours . . .", (3) "and that a great fear of you has fallen on us . . ."; (4) "we have heard how the Lord . . ."; (5) "our hearts sank and everyone's courage failed . . ."; (6) "the Lord your God is God . . . ." Rahab's statements can be understood as a concentric structure (a series of circles within each other).

The outer is Rahab's personal confession and personal response of faith in Yahweh, the true God of Israel; the inner circle offers military information that is vital to the Israelites. The report said that the Canaanites were afraid of the Israelites. And this further explains why Jericho was tightly shut up when Israel came to fight (Joshua 6). The center circle tells of the reason for the Canaanites' fear and that Rahab believed in the God of Israel. The miracle working power of God caused Rahab to look to this great Deliverer, God, for her personal salvation. Much more than that, we see how God gives encouragement to those who are on their way to winning victory. God places signposts of victory at every turn, especially in the message of Rahab.

Her former occupation was sinful, but now her faith in Yahweh has made her strong in faith and undoubtedly has changed her life. The importance of this confession makes it deserving of more than a cursory glance. This confession and her actions place her people, culture, religion, and her own life on the line. Was she a traitor to her people? Hadn't all of the Canaanites heard the story of the great God of Israel and had the opportunity to accept Him by faith? Instead, they still clung to Baal and the gods of Canaan. Instead of looking to Yahweh by faith, they feared Israel, rejected God, and held onto their religious superstitions and crude worship practices.

Some practices involved "religious" prostitution and some nations of Canaan offered children as sacrifices. Rahab's faith and good works are recognized in the New Testament in Hebrews 11:3 and James 2:25. There are many modern day African American "Rahabs," who in spite of opposition, will help humanity, will face personal danger, and will stand for the God of the Bible and His Son, Jesus Christ. Rahab asks for protection for herself and her family (vv. 12-14), and the spies promise her that all in her household will be spared when Israel overtakes Jericho.

In verses 15-21, Rahab lowers the spies from her window with a rope. So that Rahab's family can be spared from destruction, the spies have Rahab tie a scarlet cord in the window. Having escaped, the spies hide in the mountains as Rahab suggests, swim back across the Jordan River, and report back to Joshua (not the people) what has happened to them on this military intelligence operation. After hearing this report, Joshua is confident that God has truly given them victory. The spies confidently and joyfully tell Joshua, "The Lord has surely given the whole land into our hands; all the people are melting in fear because of us" (v. 24, NIV).

Spies were sent to verify the status of the psyche of the enemy. Verification is a cumulative convergence of direct and indirect confirmation, and victory follows the reduction of the elements of uncertainty in our lives. The purpose of verification is the elimination of doubt. How certain can we be that our victory is secured, accomplished, and complete? Because we are children of a faithful God, examples of God's previous acts should suffice to convince us. But God often lets us see the enemy's fear and panic as further assurance of the already completed victory. Even in the face of this conviction one may still maintain a defeatist attitude that so often keeps God's people in the wilderness without the promised divine victory. How did God help Israel gain victory? What was the process for changing their mindset from defeatist to triumphant? Their parents had been stuck in perpetual defeatism, informed by their negative experience in Egypt as slaves.

Everything that happened to them conjured up images of their servitude and bondage. In what must have been seen from heaven as the most conflicted reaction rather than face their present enemy with the resolve and determination not to return to bondage, they often attempted to return to slavery. As the saying goes, "they chose the devil they knew and ran from the one they just met." God gave them every opportunity to defeat the oppressor, but they were too consumed by their former experience to stand. Their enemy had so infected their mind that they actually considered a return to Pharaoh with all his wicked dealing as being a better choice than freedom.

A mindset of defeat will rob us of our divine possibility; it will keep us in the wilderness; and it will cripple us. This mindset of defeat will return one into bondage again and again. How do we put ourselves in the path to victory?

First we must co-operate with God to remove the slave mentality from our souls. God's main task was to redefine the Israelites' reality. Negative experience can be passed down from parents to children to become their narrative building block. However their interpretation of these events must be from the perspective of freedom and possibility. The Israelites' parents had the dubious choice of being able to return to Egypt and the bondage it held. It is not the bondage that was important but divine providence and preservation. It is not the wilderness that is the point, but the provisional care of the divine which God gives to those who are called according to the divine purpose.

The second step in working toward victory is to refocus the negative experiences of your past based on God's providential acts. See not just the fact that you were in trouble but how God intervened. Why must you do this? Continuing to rehash the negative without looking at what God did to bring us out develops psychological dependence on the negative experience. This results in the negative experience owning us rather than us owning the experience. This is why many people who complain about certain negative experiences in their lives tend to repeat them over and over again. They fail to see what God is doing and thus give power to negative experience allowing it to overpower them. The same is true for families, churches, and corporations. If one has had an experience of abuse, one may talk about the abuse, but one needs also to talk about the power of God which keeps the abuse from resulting in physical, spiritual, and even psychic annihilation.

One of the most radical acts of God to move Israel into victory was to kill all those whose sole claim to fame was the fact they had served Pharaoh and eaten the delicacies of Egypt. In a certain sense, the past must die. The past as determined and interpreted by the enemy must die.

Even Moses must die. Why? Because Moses grew up in Pharaoh's house? Does that sound heretical? It may be. But remember that Moses was raised as the grandson of Pharaoh. Though he was instrumental in his people's deliverance, he was a constant reminder of what they had left behind. It was not Moses's fault. It was who he was. If your sole claim to fame is what you did before you came out of bondage you are already defeated. Thus if you define yourself through the pain caused to you by others, you will remain a victim. Redefine yourself based on God's intention.

Many people are not comfortable when God leads them through a progressive revelation of divine purpose and will. They would rather have God bestow absolute knowledge regarding their life's direction. It is life's uncertainty that makes faith necessary, therefore "we walk by faith and not by sight" (2 Corinthians 5:7).

This is a third step toward victory. When we face challenging situations, we must remember to see past our own limiting perspective and imagination and to see God's ability to provide an alternative reality to the one we know. God cannot be confined in our reality—it is in the nature of God to transcend our reality.

How can a people caught in a false reality, of their own creation or the creation of their oppressors, overcome? How can a wilderness people become Promised Land dwellers? How can one break out into a larger atmosphere after being confined in a narrow, extremely uncomfortable box? How does one venture from familiar shores into uncertain waters confident in one's ability to navigate in greater depths without sinking? We must dare to trust the divine beyond our experiences, even if that means we need to distrust our own reality. You see if the wilderness is all you have known, it is time for you to envision what lies beyond your dry desert sand. If the rough waters are all that you have known, it is time for you to ask how you may reach calmer seas. If trouble has been your daily bread, it is time to ask for another food. Believe there is more for you; look for more and receive more.

The fourth step in working toward your victory is to keep very little baggage from the past. Note that everyone who left Egypt with Moses died except for two people–Joshua and Caleb. Why did God keep the two people who had experienced slavery alive? We know that it is because they exercised faith. But look at it again. Could it be that keeping a part of the past is important for those who must move into the future? Could it be that those who move into the future need to be reminded of where they had come from? Although the past may have proven difficult for those who experienced it, retaining history is vital for the victory of the next generation who must undertake to accomplish what was promised to its ancestors. I believe remembering the past keeps Israel connected as they transition from a wilderness people to a Promised Land people.

We run into trouble when our memory of the past outweighs our passion for the future. Vital memories of past hurts and failures keeps us grounded, but explicit details which recreate all the pain and despair holds us back. Whenever our baggage from the past outweighs our passion for the future, we cannot enter into victory. Just as it is difficult for the rich man to enter into the kingdom, so it is difficult for those who hang onto the wealth of pain the past provides to enter into healing or victory. God's Word, "forgetting the things past and pressing toward the mark of the high calling of God" (Philippians 3:13) speaks to our tendency to use the past as an albatross around our necks instead of a propeller behind our backs.

There are two things that God commanded Israel to remember about their past. First, they were to remember that they were slaves in Egypt. Second, they were to remember that God delivered them with a mighty hand from slavery. We have more details about the second than we do about the first for good reason. The first, if emphasized, has a tendency to create pathology both in terms of self-pity and in terms of vengeful spirit, neither of which is conducive to the freedom and self-realization of the oppressed person or the community.

The angry victim seldom can deal directly with the one who has caused the hurt, and this powerlessness to cope causes the hurt one to turn against those who are nearer, and even against themselves. This is precisely what Israel did over and over again with Moses until self-destructing in the wilderness. If not for the grace of God, the nation would have perished in the wilderness because of the preoccupation of the Egypt generation, with their pain in Egypt and lack of emphasis on divine providence that had delivered them and continued to keep them.

If you doubt the deadly impact of emphasizing the negative details of the past, examine failed marriages and somewhere you will find an overemphasis on the failure of the past and refusal to acknowledge the good that has sustained. Breakdowns in parent/child relationships are often attributed to someone who has overemphasized the negative details of an experience to the exclusion of divine providence. Most fallouts result from negative memories which are not connected to divine providence. Most churches fail because many people carry negative experience and rehearse the details over and over again until the whole psyche of the church is pathological and relationships have become demonized. The only way to heal this is to reintroduce divine providence and to enter into celebrative emancipation. Celebrate God. By painting your pain with a broad brush and your divine deliverance with more detail, you will release yourself from the power of your oppressor.

The fifth step toward attaining your victory is research. But research does not mean write the whole book or even find the whole answer. The Bible says "study to show yourself approved," (2 Timothy 2:15) but not until you necessarily have all the answers. The danger we face oftentimes is like that faced by doctoral students who are stuck in research. In church language, there are those who constantly pray about their needs and never take any action.

At a certain point we ought to combine prayer with evangelical action. The scouts here were not sent to spend excessive time looking at the beauty of Canaan. They were to bring back information that informed and energized the people of God for battle. Both Moses and Joshua sent out scouts to research the land, but note the difference between their strategies. Moses sends out twelve, Joshua sends two. One can speculate that Joshua remembers that out of the twelve only two came back with a good report. Here the principle runs counter-intuitive to our tendency to think that more is always better. Even Solomon says "in a multitude of counselors there is safety" (Proverbs 11:14; 24:6).

But Joshua was not in the position to play it safe. He was in a revolutionary situation. The lives of his people were at stake. In a time of spiritual or epistemic revolution the crowd is of very little help. When God is on the move there is no time for polls or for feeling the pulse of the crowd. Later in Scripture, we find another warrior, Gideon, who thought that more was better, but God cut down his army from over 30,000 to 300. We find Jesus in a crowd of over 5,000 disciples choosing 12 and out of the 12 relating most closely to 3. When God commands us to do something, a committee is unnecessary.

But here also we learn that even when God commands, we are still responsible to do some homework before jumping feet first into a struggle without divinely ordered calculation. Our Lord Himself told us to count the cost for any battle (Luke 14:28). Scouting out the enemy is meant to give us minimal exposure by revealing the enemy's mindset to us. As Paul states, "be not ignorant of Satan's devices" (2 Corinthians 2:11). Ignorance of the enemy is one of the biggest problems that we have today as Christians.

In our modern world, many of us do not have a clear understanding of the strategies of Satan. We confuse our fellow Christians with the enemy, or we fail to see the many ways in which the enemy works to hinder our walk with the Lord. While it is dangerous to focus too long on the enemy, we must not lose sight of who he is and what he wants to do. Hiding our head in the sand will not make the devil go away. Theological denials and philosophical analysis will not diminish his power, but it may serve to desensitize us to the work of the enemy thereby exposing us. As we move into battle to claim our victory, we need to be careful to understand our level of preparation. This process of discerning and gaining spiritual insight only yields its fruits to those who are willing to listen and learn—even from one's enemy.

Note that the challenges of Joshua in this passage are not unlike the challenges you and I may face in our quest for victory over circumstances in our lives. First, we must face walls put up by those who wish to protect their territory from our advancement. The challenge of territorial advancement is real even in the church. Turf protection in ministry is not unheard of. Perhaps you feel God is calling you to ministry, but members may reject and discourage you by even refusing to talk to you. Some may even be out for your spiritual head or fear the threat that you may take someone else's job. In some cases, God wants the job undertaken as we find in this text; but that doesn't make the task easy. Fear is another challenge that we face as we seek to walk in victory—our own fear and that of others. Christians sometimes fear spiritually gifted people instead of embracing them.

It is foolhardy to believe that because you have an anointing and a call in your life, or that because you are in the church you are not walking into enemy territory. He will fight. He will even use the people of God to fight you and try to discourage you. Fear breeds jealousy and envy. And you will encounter both on your way to a victorious walk.

The sixth step toward attaining spiritual victory is discernment. This spirit of discernment requires alertness. Spiritual warfare in our day and age is being waged with new and unfamiliar armaments and have taken the posture of angels of truth. In fact, they have taken on the veneer of profit. Things that used to shock us no longer disturb us. Part of the challenge then for those who seek to walk in victory is to avoid desensitization. It used to be that Christians were too sensitive to evil and saw the devil under every proverbial tree, but now they see profit—divine profit—under every shrub.

Another (seventh) step for walking in victory is to connect with those on the margin. Those who are outside the gates of institutions have much to teach us about what is possible and the state of the enemies we face on our way to victory. The spies went into the house of a woman who was considered by society to be a sinner. By Israelite standards, this woman was not to be fraternized with. Yet it was to this woman that God sent the spies. God is amazing and the divine way is never our way. God had given Israel specific instructions not to consort with whores, yet Israel must depend on a harlot for protection and safety.

Your victory may come more quickly if you accept divine networking even when people come into the network system who are not your ideal. Go to the outsiders and learn from them. There are likely people who are not members of your church who know the landscape better than you, and the Lord, in providential care, has placed them in your path to strengthen you and help you arrive at the point of victory.

If we intend to bring into fruition what God has purposed, we must be willing to metamorphose beyond our cocoon. Not only must we cross over Jordan, we will have to climb Jericho's wall into unfamiliar and sometimes dangerous territory deep in the enemy's stronghold. In fact, we may even have to speak to the enemy. Sometimes revelation of what God is doing will not become clear unless we take steps into the center of the storm. The Jordan will not part until the priest steps into it. Insight into the enemy's strategies will not emerge until we enter into Rahab's house.

The eighth step for victory is the necessity of engagement. The reason we must step into the enemy's territory or engage in spiritual battle within the enemy's camp is that revelation happens in engagement. Insight comes from action. Too many of us become stuck and expect new things to happen while we are stuck and refuse like mules to move. But it is in movement, that is faith-acts, that God's power becomes activated and efficacious for us. As long as we choose to observe from our warm bench, we will not experience true victory. We may experience wilderness victory, or transitional, or survival victory, which is not enough for dwelling in the Promised Land.

The problem with wilderness victories is that they usually focus on the preservation of our ego. But Promised Land victories are connected to inheritance. These inheritance victories cannot be attained without sustained engagement. While wilderness victories may be attained from the margins because their fruits are merely for satisfying immediate temporal desires, inheritance or Promised Land victory can only be attained through deeper penetration and more substantial engagement. The victory required for possessing the Promised Land calls us to move into the enemy's territory and sometimes tabernacle there. We must make ourselves known—our presence must be felt.

Engagement frees us from our preoccupation with failures and even successes of the past. It contemporizes our strategic orientation. Too many of us are waging Promised Land war with wilderness mentality and weaponry. The difficulty of inheritance war with wilderness equipment is that it stifles our imagination. What does imagination have to do with this? Imagination is the sister of language. Wilderness mentality or imagination creates its own language. As we notice in the story of Israel, the language in the wilderness is often a language of complaint and victimization. This is precisely the language from which God seeks to save Israel and us by giving us a permanent place. Language affects our productive ability. Thus wilderness language ossifies one's imagination and vice versa. This in turn affects our ability to function effectively as we try to achieve divine objectives. But before we can move into victory we need a new way of seeing ourselves. The new imagination may sometimes be given impetus by those who do not even belong to our own circles as we find here in the words of Rahab.

It is important to take note that in the walk to victory sometimes requires that we work anonymously. We do not know the names of the spies. Stepping in does not always mean all the clamor for self-aggrandizement. The victory may not necessarily translate into what the world perceives as glory, but Promised Land victory has more extensive range both in history and in eternity. Let us be sure of this point. It is the intention of God to give us victory, to aid us in our walk into victory over all the challenges in life that we face.

It is God's intention to grant us victory over all that seeks to keep us in the wilderness as perpetual wanderers. God wants to take us into a place where we can not only smell victory but see it before it even comes to pass. That was the case here. These scouts saw fear in the face of the enemy and experienced victory before they fought, but they still needed to move in. Our triumph is more than for ourselves, it is for the reign of the most High; it embraces the very being of God. Our victory belongs ultimately to God. In this case we should not fear divine anonymity but rather embrace it. In the glory of God our own glorification becomes fulfilled.

Rahab, who also manufactured and dyed linen, secretly housed the two spies whom Joshua sent to explore Jericho and helped them escape by hiding them in stalks of flax on her roof (Joshua 2:6). Rahab sent the king's messengers on a false trail, and then let the two spies down the outside wall by a rope through the window of her house (Joshua 2:15). When the Israelites captured Jericho, they spared the house with the scarlet cord in the window—a sign that a friend of God's people lived within. Rahab, therefore, along with her father, her mother, her brothers, and all her father's household, was spared. Apparently, she and her family were later brought into the nation of Israel. Matthew refers to Rahab as the wife of Salmon (Ruth 4:20-21; Matthew 1:5; Luke 3:32). Their son, Boaz, married Ruth and became the father of Obed, the grandfather of Jesse, and the great-grandfather of David. Thus, a Canaanite harlot became part of the lineage of King David out of which the Messiah came (Matthew 1:5).

It is significant to note that the Canaanites were a proud Black people and that the line of Jesus Christ included two Gentile Black women: Rahab and also Tamar, the wife of Judah (see Matthew 1:3 and Genesis 38). This is perhaps an early sign that God's grace and forgiveness is extended to all, that it is not limited by nationality or the nature of a person's sins. The Scriptures do not tell us how Rahab, who came out of a culture where harlotry and idolatry were acceptable, recognized Jehovah as the one true God. But her insights recorded in Joshua 2:9-11 leave no doubt that she did so.

This Canaanite woman's declaration of faith led the writer of the epistle to the Hebrews to cite Rahab as one of the heroines of faith (Hebrews 11:31), while James commended her as an example of one who has been justified by works (James 2:25). According to rabbinic tradition, Rahab was one of the four most beautiful women in the world and was the ancestor of eight prophets, including Jeremiah and the Prophetess Huldah.

Chapter Six

THE VICTORY
OF JOSEPH

BASED ON GENESIS 37:3-4, 17b-28; 41:14-16, 25-40

Genesis 37:3-4

Now Israel loved Joseph more than all his children, because he was the son of his old age: and he made him a coat of many colours. ⁴ And when his brethren saw that their father loved him more than all his brethren, they hated him, and could not speak peaceably unto him.

Genesis 17b-28

And the man said, They are departed hence; for I heard them say, Let us go to Dothan. And Joseph went after his brethren, and found them in Dothan. ¹⁸ And when they saw him afar off, even before he came near unto them, they conspired against him to slay him.¹⁹ And they said one to another, Behold, this dreamer cometh. ²⁰ Come now therefore, and let us slay him, and cast him into some pit, and we will say, Some evil beast hath devoured him: and we shall see what will become of his dreams. ²¹ And Reuben heard it, and he delivered him out of their hands; and said, Let us not kill him. ²² And Reuben said unto them, Shed no blood, but cast him into this pit that is in the wilderness, and lay no hand upon him; that he might rid him out of their hands, to deliver him to his father again. ²³ And it came to pass, when Joseph was come unto his brethren, that they stripped Joseph out of his coat, his coat of many colours that was on him; ²⁴ And they took him, and cast him into a pit: and the pit was empty, there was no water in it. ²⁵ And they sat down to eat bread: and they lifted up their eyes and looked, and, behold, a company of Ishmaelites came from Gilead with their camels bearing spicery and balm and myrrh, going to carry it down to Egypt. ²⁶ And Judah said unto his brethren, What profit is it if we slay our brother, and conceal his blood? ²⁷ Come, and let us sell him to the Ishmaelites, and let not our hand be upon him; for he is our brother and our flesh. And his brethren were content. ²⁸ Then there passed by Midianites merchantmen; and they drew and lifted up

Joseph out of the pit, and sold Joseph to the Ishmaelites for twenty pieces of silver: and they brought Joseph into Egypt.

Genesis 41:14-16

Then Pharaoh sent and called Joseph, and they brought him hastily out of the dungeon: and he shaved himself, and changed his raiment, and came in unto Pharaoh.[15] And Pharaoh said unto Joseph, I have dreamed a dream, and there is none that can interpret it: and I have heard say of thee, that thou canst understand a dream to interpret it. [16] And Joseph answered Pharaoh, saying, It is not in me: God shall give Pharaoh an answer of peace.

Genesis 41:25-40

And Joseph said unto Pharaoh, The dream of Pharaoh is one: God hath shewed Pharaoh what he is about to do. [26] The seven good kine are seven years; and the seven good ears are seven years: the dream is one. [27] And the seven thin and ill favoured kine that came up after them are seven years; and the seven empty ears blasted with the east wind shall be seven years of famine.[34] Let Pharaoh do this, and let him appoint officers over the land, and take up the fifth part of the land of Egypt in the seven plenteous years. [35] And let them gather all the food of those good years that come, and lay up corn under the hand of Pharaoh, and let them keep food in the cities. [36] And that food shall be for store to the land against the seven years of famine, which shall be in the land of Egypt; that the land perish not through the famine. [37] And the thing was good in the eyes of Pharaoh, and in the eyes of all his servants. [38] And Pharaoh said unto his servants, Can we find such a one as this is, a man in whom the Spirit of God is? [39] And Pharaoh said unto Joseph, Forasmuch as God hath shewed thee all this, there is none so discreet and wise as thou art: [40] Thou shalt be over my house, and according unto thy word shall all my people be ruled: only in the throne will I be greater than thou.

The story of Joseph is familiar to every one who has read the Hebrew Testament. It tells of how one child overcame adversities, kept his faith in God's destiny for him and of his ultimate triumph. It also shows how God can accomplish His purpose for us even when our foolishness threatens to undo us. In this chapter, we shall look at various hindrances which may threaten to undo our divinely ordered success and how to overcome them.

There are several hindrances which we find in the preliminary narratives of Joseph's life. Our relationship with our parents, as psychologists have so often told us, has an enormous impact on our ability to handle crises. It may contribute to orientation to victory as well as serve as a hindrance to attaining that victory. Thus our parental relationship is a two-edged sword. To gain victory, many of us must overcome the baggage our primary caregivers laid upon us which held consequences they did not anticipate. Joseph was blessed by God, yet he carried the generational problem of his father's house.

The problem of favoritism which led his father to create enmity between Joseph and his brothers was nipping at Joseph's heels and forced him into exile. God willed it so, but that does not excuse Jacob for setting his son up for the hatred of his siblings. There was a generational problem in the house of Israel which threatened to undo the destiny of his son. It is the problem of partiality and favoritism. Sarah had kicked out Hagar, Rebekah had lied for Jacob and now Jacob showed open favoritism to one of his children.

It seems that Jacob (Israel) never grasped the depth of the disastrous consequences of showing favoritism among children. How easily he had forgotten that his entire life had been changed because of his mother's open favoritism of him over his brother Esau. Israel must have inherited this trait from Rebekah. Though unlike his mother, Israel was not as malicious in his attempt to help his favored son rise to a position of greatness. Yet he was more open with his feelings of favoritism, and thus set the children against one another. Joseph knew that he was favored and was not exempt from the childish tendency to flaunt it. It was this fatherly doting which encouraged Joseph to work towards a victorious and successful life and served well to improve his future.

The path to success may also be imperilled by the rise of pride resulting in the premature reach for what one believes to be one's birthright. We find that Jacob's love for Joseph created a certain immaturity which led him into trouble with his brothers. Yet no amount of failure on the part of his father or his brothers was gong to prevent Joseph from achieving what he knew God had called him to achieve. How did Joseph get to this point of victory? What are some principles that led him to triumph over his adversities? *Love in the family even when imperfectly expressed is still the foundation for future victories.* Though Joseph's brothers may have despised him, he knew that he was loved. His strong sense of who he was came from the love expressed by his father. Familial love empowers human beings. Though Jacob's love was imperfectly shown, it was a pure love.

Joseph's story is one of perseverance and of God's divine protection. Like his uncle, Esau, Joseph had the ability to forgive and overcome the hurt of betrayal, and he had faith in God to restore and redeem. *As Jacob's favorite son (Genesis 37:3-4) Joseph, through God, must develop a forgiving spirit.* We see this display of magnanimity towards his brothers. Clearly, Israel (Jacob) favored his young son, born to him while an old man and the offspring of the wife he loved most, Rachel. Perhaps Jacob bestowed upon Joseph the love he could no longer share with Rachel after her death. His favoritism did not go unnoticed by the other sons. It would have been, in fact, impossible for them not to notice the "coat of many colours" Joseph donned as a gift from their father.

The garment set Joseph apart from his brothers. The coat was likely a sort of decorative, ceremonial robe. Not only did the robe designate Joseph as his father's favorite, but it also made performing manual labor in the robe an impossibility. Joseph's brothers labored in the fields while he paraded around in a beautiful, ornate garment. At age 17, Joseph could not understand the contempt that brewed and festered in the hearts of his brothers.

To make matters worse, Joseph had two dreams in which his brothers were in a position subordinate to him. He was naive enough to tell his brothers about the dream. Naturally, they did not respond favorably. His naivete prompted him to report his brothers' ill behavior to their father. Joseph may have been drawing nearer to his father's heart, but he was swiftly alienating himself from the hearts of his brothers. The spirit that caused Joseph to bounce back from adversity must have been present even at that young age. His positive spirit likely made him more attractive than his brothers, even to their father. Perhaps the brothers should have looked at the positive aspects of Joseph's personality to discover what made him so likeable. Joseph was like a shining star who stood out from the rest of them. Instead of brushing the dust from their own stars so they could shine brighter, the brothers chose to extinguish Joseph's shining star.

One must develop a sense of vision and purpose if one is to have victory. *The third principle we find which propels Joseph to divine victory is his clear vision of his place in the scheme of God's work.* Despite the adversity of the conspiracy he faced, Joseph never lost his sense of divine purpose. This conspiracy is revealed even more clearly in his brothers' response to the favor heaped upon him. Rather than examine themselves or even confront their father, the brothers pointed to Joseph as the source of the problem. Perhaps they felt that getting rid of Joseph would also rid them of the jealousy and anger they felt at their father's selfish behavior.

While Israel was undeniably biased in his treatment of Joseph, it does not appear that his favoritism caused as much harm as did Rebekah's misdeed. The brothers did not consider their deeds long enough to determine if the real problem outweighed the costs. Their jealousy of him became even more obvious as they sarcastically referred to him as "the dreamer." They plotted to kill him as he walked innocently toward them. One of the brothers, Reuben (or Judah), convinced them not to kill him. Then, like common muggers, Joseph's brothers stripped him of his precious coat and threw him into an empty pit. As his physical body went into that pit, it is certain that his spirit fell into its own pit.

One moment he was the favored son, wearing a beautiful multicolored coat. In the next moment he was surrounded by darkness where the bright colors of his coat could not have been seen, even if his brothers hadn't taken it away from him. Joseph could not know it at that moment, but God was already making provision for him—a lesson Joseph would learn many times in his life. Betrayal can demoralize us, especially betrayal by family members and close friends (vv. 25-28). How the feelings of jealousy, anger, and resentment must have collected in the brothers' hearts over the years! After throwing their younger brother into an empty, waterless pit, they sat down to eat! It was then that they saw a caravan of Ishmaelites coming from Gilead with goods they were exporting to Egypt.

The brothers realized they could get rid of Joseph without having his blood on their hands, plus, they made 20 pieces of silver from his sale. They wanted to be rid of him but not bad enough to kill him. They still had some conscience left. They lifted their brother from the pit and sold him to the Midianite traders. So that Israel would in no way suspect them of being party to Joseph's disappearance, they put goat's blood on Joseph's coat. Upon seeing the bloodied garment, Israel assumed his son was killed by a wild animal.

As he embarked upon his journey to Egypt with a group of strangers, young Joseph must have wondered how his life could change so drastically. He likely thought over the events of the day, and of his life, searching for a reason that might explain his brothers' cruel actions. Joseph had no way of knowing his sale into slavery would be but the first of many injustices he would suffer.

The stories of Rebekah, Jacob, Esau, Joseph, and his brothers help us to understand the cyclical nature of dysfunctional relationships. Rebekah chose one son as her favorite. That son later designated one of his own sons as his favorite. Unless something is done to break a destructive cycle, unhealthy patterns can continue within families for generations. It is important for families, including the Christian family, to demonstrate love for one another based on the love our heavenly Father has shown us, not based on external circumstances. Many external factors cause people to respond to others with favor including physical appearance, financial status, education, and social prominence.

Some people earn favor (or disfavor) based on factors beyond their control, such as race, ethnicity, and gender. Fortunately, God's favor is not dependent upon anything but God's goodness. God's favor cannot be earned. God loves us and provides for us because we are His. Knowing this, some believers look upon others with envy and resentment, feeling that the heavenly Father has given a "coat of many colors" to someone to show that He loves them more. Nothing could be further from the truth!

Perhaps there is a way you can help a child feel special. There are many children in foster residences who will never experience the kind of favored status Joseph enjoyed in his father's house. Every child deserves to feel special. Find such a facility in your area and discover a way you can have an ongoing, meaningful relationship with such a child or group of children. With many schools opening over the coming weeks, you may be able to help a child start the school year feeling very special. If you have children of your own, perhaps you can spend more time with all of them, helping them all know that they are important and precious to you.

The famine that befell Egypt during Joseph's time was brought on by drought. Some famines lasted years, forcing the people to eat things such as wild vines, animal heads, garbage, dung, and even human flesh (see 2 Kings 6:26-31). Pharaoh, the title used for the kings of ancient Egypt, means "great house." During ancient times, pharaohs had five "great names," which they assumed on the day they became king. It was not considered proper etiquette or form to use their powerful names directly; therefore they came to be called simply Pharaoh. The term became a popular name for kings about 1500 B.C. An ancient pharaoh was an absolute ruler. Justice was very often defined according to what the pharaoh loved and hated.

The fourth principle we learn from the life of Joseph is that one who will be victorious in the sight of God must maintain purity and integrity. Joseph probably experienced more tragedy than do most of us in a lifetime. After being sold into slavery by his own brothers, Joseph was bought by Potiphar, an officer in Pharaoh's army. Joseph's good looks attracted the attention of Potiphar's wife.

Because he rejected her advances, she falsely accused him of trying to attack her in order to have him imprisoned. For the second time in his short life, Joseph was suffering for the positive qualities he possessed. Even after he was imprisoned, Joseph suffered from the negligence of a fellow prisoner. Joseph interpreted the dreams of two fellow prisoners. One prisoner had promised to remember Joseph upon his release, but he did not. Joseph's desire to obtain freedom seemed hopeless.

The fifth principle that one learns from Joseph is to continue to do good in spite of failure on the part of those he sought to help and actually did help. He was sold when he took food to his brothers. He was accused when he attempted to protect the dignity of another man's wife. While in prison the Lord used him to open doors for another. He remained in the will of God even though this same one for whom he opened the door took too long to open that same door for Joseph. In spite of all Joseph's bad experiences, the Lord had not forgotten His servant Joseph. Joseph had probably spent many days pondering the why and how of his fateful circumstance. He knew he had done nothing wrong to be sentenced to prison. The butler's promise to help in his release had probably faded in Joseph's mind as he sat in prison day after day. It would be two more years before the butler remembered his promise to young Joseph. While Joseph was incarcerated, God's providential hand moved in through a dream Pharaoh had but could not understand. It was then that the butler remembered his promise to Joseph. The butler told Pharaoh about Joseph's ability to interpret dreams, and Pharaoh summoned him. Joseph's remarkable personal qualities can be seen in reading the text.

The sixth principle which we learn from Joseph is to keep using the gift we have been given because our help and road to victory lies in the gift which God has deposited within us. Joseph's gift was interpretation of dreams. He did not try to impress Pharaoh with his understanding of mathematics or geometry. That would have been a failure, for the Pharaoh probably knew more than him in that area. If we remain faithful, God will bring into our lives those who need the particular giftedness that God in His divine wisdom has deposited within us. When Joseph was called upon he was brought out from his cell hastily, but Joseph still took the time to shave and change clothes! Most people in Joseph's circumstance would probably have come in Pharaoh's presence looking shabby in an attempt to gain the ruler's sympathy. Joseph chose to look his best. His undying optimism directed him not to throw away his one chance for release from prison. After Pharaoh explained that he needed Joseph to interpret his dream, Joseph could have used this opportunity to insure his release by promising Pharaoh a favorable interpretation. Joseph did not give credit for interpretation to himself. The answer lay in God, not in Joseph. Yet Joseph was certain that God would give Pharaoh "an answer of peace." God would reveal the dream's meaning to Joseph so that Pharaoh would be at peace and no longer confused over the dream's meaning.

The seventh principle we learn from Joseph is that we will be victorious if we make up our mind to give the glory for the victory to God. Many of us fail before we start because we have predetermined to show off the victory as ours, thus we hinder our own progress. For God will not share His glory with another. As he revealed the dream's meaning, Joseph continued to name God as the source. God gave the dream's meaning to Joseph so that he could help Pharaoh understand. Pharaoh's dreams all held the same theme and the same meaning. The seven ears of corn and the seven fat cows represented the seven years of plenty that would soon grace the land. The seven empty ears and seven thin cows represented the seven years of famine that would follow the seven years of plenty. The years of plenty would be bountiful but the years of famine would be very lean years.

As Joseph unraveled Pharaoh's dreams, he also seized the opportunity to provide the ruler with a plan of action—undoubtedly a plan that would include Joseph. His quick thinking can be somewhat paralleled by the actions of Moses' sister in Exodus 2:7. She offered to find a Hebrew woman to nurse Moses—now claimed by Pharaoh's daughter as her own—thereby making a way for his own mother to be his nursemaid. In the case of Joseph, his planning skills and ingenuity were not unnoticed by Pharaoh. He not only exhibited the qualities of a spiritual man, but a practical man as well. Pharaoh probably sat and listened as Joseph unveiled a plan of action for the land. The years of slavery and incarceration had likely worn away the polish of the privileged life Joseph once lived. The naivete of the boy who shared his dreams and flaunted his coat before his brothers was gone. The lean years had made Joseph both a man of faith and a man of action. He could now look at a problem and offer a practical, workable solution. Undoubtedly, Joseph wanted to impact Pharaoh favorably in order to be released from jail. Probably nothing would please Joseph more than an opportunity to prevent suffering because he had suffered much in a short period of time. Joseph's years of suffering apparently had not diminished his desire to serve the Lord and those around him.

The eighth principle we learn from Joseph is that it is important to be in a position where there is only one option—God's option. Joseph's opportunity came when Pharaoh asked where an overseer such as Joseph had described could be found. It is likely that Pharaoh asked the question already knowing the answer. Egypt may have suffered a terrible fate had it not been for Joseph.

But there is intimation that there is another (ninth) principle to be learned—Joseph was always open to the spirit. The Spirit of the Lord (Hebrew *ruach*) was in Joseph. God's Spirit inspired and prepared him to assume a position of greatness. This marks the first biblical reference in which God's Spirit is credited with an inner gift of understanding. Joseph's giftedness was so profound that even Pharaoh, a nonbeliever, could not ignore the power of God in him. Pharaoh could not have known of the loyalty Joseph demonstrated when he rejected the advances of Potiphar's wife. He could not have seen Joseph's willingness to help others as he helped two fellow prisoners understand their fate. God's providence had made a way for Joseph's qualities of loyalty, trustworthiness, honesty, and optimism. He probably never imagined a position such as he was given by Pharaoh! So very often, what the Lord has in store for us is so much greater than what we had imagined or hoped for. Joseph was placed in charge of the house and affairs of

Pharaoh, second only to him throughout the land.

The tenth and final principle is that Joseph gained this victory because God favored him in spite of his family, in spite of early immaturity, in spite of what happened to him. Those who win divine victory do so because they seek divine favor, not human acceptance. This favor was so clearly upon him that even those who held him captive saw it and had to acknowledge it.

In Genesis 39:3-5 we read:

"And his master saw that the Lord was with him and that the Lord made all he did to prosper in his hand. So Joseph found favor in his sight, and served him. Then he made him overseer of his house, and all that he had he put under his authority. So it was, from the time that he had made him overseer of his house and all that he had, that the Lord blessed the Egyptian's house for Joseph's sake; and the blessing of the Lord was on all that he had in the house and in the field." (See also Genesis 39:21-22).

It is the gracious acts of God toward us that form the foundation for our move to victory. As God promised to give the Israelites favor in the sight of their oppressors (Exodus 3:20-21), God has promised His people favor in the sight of those who persecute them and that our labor will not be in vain. Part of God's favor to Joseph was to preserve his life as well as his spirit (Job 10:12). Only by the grace of God and His divine favor are we able to gain our victory. It is through the favor of the Lord that we are exalted.

Psalm 89:17 says, "For You are the glory of their strength, And in Your favor our horn is exalted." Thus for us to be victorious we must seek good, and this earnest pursuit of good predisposes us to find favor in the sight of God. Joseph sought good even when He could have gotten away with bad (Proverbs 11:27). O, that you and I will find favor in the sight of the Lord. Indeed we have found favor. We who believe in the Messiah have entered into the year of His favor. We will survive the betrayal of our brothers and even our sisters; we will survive the imperfection of our parents; we will survive false accusations and imprisonments because God has favored us. Victory is ours because the light of the favor of the God of Israel has shone upon us in the face of our Lord Jesus Christ.

Chapter Seven

VICTORY OVER BOUNDARIES

BASED ON MATTHEW 8:5-13

Matthew 8:5-13

And when Jesus was entered into Capernaum, there came unto him a centurion, beseeching him, ⁶And saying, Lord, my servant lieth at home sick of the palsy, grievously tormented. ⁷And Jesus saith unto him, I will come and heal him. ⁸The centurion answered and said, Lord, I am not worthy that thou shouldest come under my roof: but speak the word only, and my servant shall be healed. ⁹For I am a man under authority, having soldiers under me; and I say to this man, Go, and he goeth; and to another, Come, and he cometh; and to my servant, Do this, and he doeth it. ¹⁰When Jesus heard it, he marvelled, and said to them that followed, Verily I say unto you, I have not found so great faith, no, not in Israel. ¹¹And I say unto you, That many shall come from the east and west, and shall sit down with Abraham, and Isaac, and Jacob, in the kingdom of heaven. ¹²But the children of the kingdom shall be cast out into outer darkness: there shall be weeping and gnashing of teeth. ¹³And Jesus said unto the centurion, Go thy way; and as thou hast believed, so be it done unto thee. And his servant was healed in the selfsame hour.

Jesus came to break down barriers between human beings. The world is full of problems that cause us to burn within like a fire. There are many things which can easily create a wall of division between us and other human beings. The church continually preaches the good news about Jesus to all, yet there seems to be more barriers raised up between people now more than ever. Some even use the Gospel to justify the division among human beings. In fact, we do not have to look too far back in history to see how some have used the Gospel to create nearly unbridgeable chasms between groups. It has been said that the "11 o'clock hour on Sunday morning is the most seg-regated hour in America." We see division and separation in various places of worship all over the country.

If one were to walk around our cities and observe the devotions and worship of Christians, one may be tempted to think, because of our division and our unwillingness to get together, that in our temples, churches, altars, shrines, and various monuments that we do indeed worship separate gods. Great discussions are often held to understand this phenomena of division. But in many cases, these conversations forget about the good news of Jesus which is meant to tear down walls and break down boundaries. The solution to division among people is proclaiming the true God through Jesus Christ His Son.

The Scriptures are clear that God is the Creator of all things including people, for He "made of one blood all nations of men for to dwell on all the face of the earth, and hath determined the times before appointed, and the bounds of their habitation" (Acts 17:26). "One blood" refers to the creation of the first humans, Adam and Eve. From Adam, God made the nations of all people to live on the earth. Since no person or group originated independently from other human beings, this contradicts the boast that certain people are superior to others. Every person is made by God and is a descendant from a common ancestor. God has also appointed the time and place in which every person lives (v. 26b). He has wisely given to everyone their place to dwell. God created all humankind in order "that they should seek the Lord, if haply they might feel after him, and find him, though he be not far from every one of us" (v. 27). God desires that every person from every nation should seek Him. He wants everyone to know of His existence and His character. God has made it possible for all nations, though living in different regions and climates, to have the opportunity to know God the Creator. By design, God created all people and we all are responsible for seeking Him. We cannot be whole unless we know and have a relationship with God.

Even though God is transcendent and it is beyond our ability to completely understand Him, He seeks to enter into relationship with us. But we have broken our relationship with God. A wall has gone up. A demarcation, or boundary, has been instituted. There has developed a chasm which we cannot cross on our own. We cannot bridge this gap by the flight of our imagination. We cannot mend this rupture by our religious superstitions. No, we cannot by the mere effort of our own searching, as Job said, find God (Job 11:7). As human beings, even our prayers fail to reach God. For as Isaiah says "the Lord is not deaf that he cannot hear your prayers but your iniquity has separated between you and your God" (Isaiah 59:1-2, paraphrased).

Though God formed us and continually sustains us, we drift in a sea of separation because we have fallen. We are like a trickling spring cut off from its original fountain. Our lives continue from moment to moment only by the sheer power of His original mercy, adrift upon the murky sea of our iniquity and rebellion. We live, move, and have our being, but we fail to have "His" being. In the words of the prophet "we are like sheep that have gone astray, we have turned every one to his own way" (Isaiah 53:6a). We are lost.

There is barrier between us and God. Our sinful nature separates us from God because we have become fundamentally flawed in our divine character. In our world today, many modernists and even post-modernists, as some call themselves, think that we have come so far that we do not need to talk about humanity's separation from God. Some think that because modern human beings do not set up idols of wood for worship at their homes that somehow we are closer to God than those who do. But our separation from God is seen in our worship of creation in place of the Creator. Our very inventions may serve to separate us from God. Our modern idols, careers, money, and hobbies to name a few, like the idols of the ancients, continue to cause separation between us and our divine destiny. We, like our fore-parents, have set up our limited rationality in place of divine wisdom. Some people seem to worship ignorance, while others worship rationalistic intelligence. Thus, we continue to be separated from our God.

Unless this gap is bridged, we are headed for serious eternal trouble.

Sometimes our ignorance may have led us to walk away from God, but God demands that we change our way of thinking because there is now a way back to Him. Yes! There is a force that pulls our isolated stream upward. A life-line has been thrown into our murky sea to draw us into life. This is good news. Now those who turn around can see the light. Those who repent can now be reoriented. God is commanding all people to come back. The bad news is that they cannot come on their own; the good news is that God has provided a way for them to come. The bad news is that humanity is subject to judgment for separating from God; the good news is that God knows that and has made a way. Neither you nor I have to suffer the judgment of God, if we will only lay hold of God's life-line—Jesus, the Messiah. He is the Saviour from our prodigality, the fountain which re-energizes our streams. By His own death, He broke the barrier between us and God. By His resurrection, God has conquered the greatest sin affecting our separation and even death. Not only did Jesus die for the sins of all people, He rose again to show that no longer should you and I be on the other side of chasm, unable to get back to God. Ephesians. 2:11-19 states:

"Wherefore remember, that ye being in time past Gentiles in the flesh, who are called Uncircumcision by that which is called the Circumcision in the flesh made by hands; [12]That at that time ye were without Christ, being aliens from the commonwealth of Israel, and strangers from the covenants of promise, having no hope, and without God in the world: [13]But now in Christ Jesus ye who sometimes were far off are made nigh by the blood of Christ. [14]For he is our peace, who hath made both one, and hath broken down the middle wall of partition between us; [15]Having abolished in his flesh the enmity, even the law of commandments contained in ordinances; for to make in himself of twain one new man, so making peace; [16]And that he might reconcile both unto God in one body by the cross, having slain the enmity thereby: [17]And came and preached peace to you which were afar off, and to them that were nigh. [18]For through him we both have access by one Spirit unto the Father. [19]Now therefore ye are no more strangers and foreigners, but fellow citizens with the saints, and of the household of God . . . ."

The life of Jesus offers us the opportunity of immediate re-entrance into the presence of God as children no longer separated from our eternal Parent (Leviticus 6:30; 2 Chronicles 29:24; Ezekiel 45:20; Romans 5:11; Romans 8:32). Will you hear Him? Will you reach out and touch Him? True life and peace with God is available only through the person of God's Son Jesus, the Messiah. To receive life and be reconciled with God, we must exercise faith in God's provision for us. We must believe that this One who comes from God—Jesus, who died and who rose—is for us. We must embrace Him as Emmanuel. This call is not a call to more religious politeness which results in procrastinated faith, but a call to radical faith in the good will of God towards men. The good news is that you and I no longer need to be separated from God; we can be reconciled to Him. We were fenced in, enclosed by our self-imposed prison, but now that Jesus has come, we are offered an opportunity to be free.

Several passages in the New Testament point to the breaking down of the barrier between God and humanity. In Romans 5:10, we read "For if, when we were enemies, we were reconciled to God by the death of his Son, much more, being reconciled, we shall be saved by his life." Second Corinthians 5:18-19 teaches us "And all things are of God, who hath reconciled us to himself by Jesus Christ, and hath given to us the ministry of reconciliation; To wit, that God was in Christ, reconciling the world unto himself, not imputing their trespasses unto them; and hath committed unto us the word of reconciliation." The good news is that God's love has overtaken our passive and active hatred. Through Jesus, we are no longer enemies of God because of our iniquities, but children of the Most High.

But it is not just between God and human beings that a barrier exists. There is also a barrier which has developed between human beings. We have developed many pervading attitudes which have divided one group from another. This opposition which some people have toward one another comes from our inability to relate to God. Having been given an open invitation into peace with God, we must accept, for this peace with God also is the key to peace with humanity. How many times are people ready to hear the Gospel, but some old wound distorts the new message and they turn away? Most of the time, this wound results from our distortion of the nature of God and His relationship with other human beings. Ignorance of God often leads to ignorance of humanity. This ignorance leads us to categorize others and then to victimize them. Thus, we find that as we are separated from God, we are also separated from each other. But the simple fact is that because Jesus has brought the good news of reconciliation with God, there can be reconciliation between human beings. Because God is the One who gives life, breath, and all things to all creatures, it follows that God has already created the material basis for breaking down all the boundaries between human beings.

While the Bible does call us God's handiwork or workmanship, it lumps all of us together in sin thus equalizing us at our high and at our low (Romans 3:23; Ephesians 2:10). Therefore, there was and is no justification in the claim that some groups are inherently superior to others. The Greeks were not superior to the barbarians, nor the Romans to the Carthaginians, or the Egyptians to the Ethiopians, or the Jews to the Gentiles. Similarly, there is no justification in these beliefs of superiority today. Consequently, whether in the ancient times or present day, there is no room for the idea of racial superiority at all.

The same Creator, the Almighty God, created us all equally. Our separation and division one from another is the result of sin. Not only does ignorance create a demarcation between us, greed also separates us one from another. Because we misplace our priorities by putting things before God and human beings, we thicken the walls which divide us. By seeking to become popular with people or focusing on things which we think will preserve us, we step over each other and thicken the boundaries. The more distant human beings feel from one another, the more resentful we seem to become of them.

In Matthew 8:5-13, Jesus took the opportunity to break not only the boundary that separates one group from another and human beings from God, but also the barrier which blocks humanity from physical wholeness. This story takes place as Jesus comes to a place named Capernaum. The name is Hebrew in origin and is a combination of *kaphar* and *nachuwm*. The first word refers to a walled-in place or a place of silence. The second part of the name *nacham*, pronounced **naw-kham'**, simply means to breathe a sigh of relief. It can also mean compassion and consolation. Thus, as Jesus was going to the walled place a man met him, a Roman centurion.

The centurion symbolized the division between the people of Israel and their colonial masters, the Romans. This man was part of the group that was meant to brutalize the people if they even thought about freedom. Matthew places this story right after the story of the leper who beseeched Jesus to heal him. Like the leper, this man was separated from the community in which he lived; one by birth, the other by circumstance. The centurion represented all of that which caused Israel pain. The wall was up; it was cultural, religious, racial, professional, and political. The boundaries between this centurion and the people among whom he lived was as thick as the wall which protected Jerusalem.

The very presence of Jesus serves to soften the walls we have built up. This proud Roman who probably saw the people of Israel as troublemakers now turns to Jesus for help. His servant was sick. Sickness is our common human condition. It is one of those things that transcends class and gender, race and culture, and religious orientation. Yet, many times it may serve to divide even the most committed from each other. But here, it is this need which brings this man to Jesus. Interestingly, it is not his own sickness but that of someone dear to him, one of his servants. We read that the centurion came near to Jesus. He implored Jesus to cross his built up walls and meet his need. This centurion had a servant which was probably epileptic or paralyzed. The use of the Greek word *ballo,* pronounced **bal'-lo,** meaning throw, and the word *paralutikos,* pronounced **par-al-oo-tee-kos',** which refers to the dissolving of the muscles, implies that this sickness was terribly excessive. The state of the patient as servant was probably painful and tormented. How many times do our boundaries keep us from getting the help we need? How many times do the walls we have built through pride keep us from going to each other? How often do the philosophical walls we have built even keep us from coming to the Lord for our needs? But thanks be to God for Jesus Christ who breaks walls.

To break down our boundaries and walls, we must be willing to come to Jesus. But notice that Jesus was already on His way into the city before this man came to Him. As a Jew, Jesus could have refused to become involved in this man's problem. He could have come up with all kinds of wall-building reasons why this Gentile and Roman could not be helped. Instead, Jesus used the opportunity to break down the walls between this man and his God, and between this man and his Jewish neighbors. When the man pleaded with Jesus, He responded immediately making this outsider a priority in God's work.

Note the words of Jesus "I will come and heal him." Jesus seems to be saying, "I see your wall, but I will come to you anyway. I see the walls that traditions have built between you and I, but I will come to you anyway. I see the walls that you have put up for fear of being hurt, but I will come to you anyway. There is boundary between you and your neighbor, I am willing to come near and heal that breach." This is Jesus, the breaker of boundaries, the One who bridges gaps. He said, "I will come and heal him." Not only is Jesus healing the breach between this man and God and between this man and his Israelite neighbors, He is breaking the walls between this man and his servant. He is walking through the wall, speaking through the wall, reaching through the wall into this man's heart. That is Jesus for you. That is the Son of the living God. Note that Jesus does all of this before the man even makes an explicit statement of what he believes about Jesus.

What are the walls around you, your family, your friends, your co-workers? Hear Jesus as He says, "I will come and heal you." I will come and remove the walls which have developed in your relationships." Can you hear Him beside you as He whispers, "I will come and heal you." He will come over your walls. He is willing to come over your walls and meet your need. There may be walls in your life that have kept you on the outside. There may be walls that keep you from developing a lasting relationship both with God and other people. If Jesus can break down the walls between human beings and God, He can surely break the walls between you and your environment, between you and your hope, between you and your loved ones, and yes, between you and your enemies.

In verses 8 and 9, the centurion looks at Jesus and says, "Lord, I am not worthy that thou shouldest come under my roof: but speak the word only, and my servant shall be healed. For I am a man under authority, having soldiers under me: and I say to this man, Go, and he goeth; and to another, Come, and he cometh; and to my servant, Do this, and he doeth it." It is true that lack of self-esteem does build walls between us and our future. Jesus came to give us back our self-confidence based on God's power, not on some sort of arrogation of power. But in this man's case he is not writhing in self pity. Rather his response derives from a proportionate understanding of himself.

People in high places usually allow their pride to build up walls of separation between them and others. For example, those who were your friends may change when they get a promotion. This is not the case here. Here, we see a man who has been stripped of all his human pride in the presence of the Lord Jesus Christ. Oh, how humility will help tear down the walls in our hearts! First, the centurion that he could not break this barrier. Second, he realized that only the word spoken by the eternal Son of God, One with divine authority could break his walls. The centurion said, "speak the word and my servant shall be healed." The word of Jesus can heal our breaches. Jesus alone has this authority to speak to the spiritual forces which fragment and divide us. In order for the boundaries between the centurion and his God and the people to be healed, he had to come to Jesus, acknowledge Jesus in humility, and affirm the authority of Jesus.

In response, "When Jesus heard it, He marvelled, and said to them that followed, 'Verily I say unto you, I have not found so great faith, no, not in Israel" (v. 10). The use of the Greek word *thaumazo,* pronounced **thou-mad'-zo,** means to be filled with wonder. Remember that as a human being Jesus was Jewish. The idea that a Gentile can have genuine faith was not easily accepted among the people of Israel. But to God, faith is a wonderful thing. By implication, this passage is saying that Jesus was filled with admiration for this Gentile, this outsider. Imagine how this expression of admiration may have affected the disciples who have been taught to loathe the Gentiles. Surely this expression of admiration from the divine One in their midst must have served to break down the barrier which existed between them. But note that it was not just empty admiration, it was wonder resulting from the man's expression of faith.

In one sweeping statement, Jesus broke down what may have been their highest religious wall. This man's faith was stronger than theirs. The stereotypes of Gentiles being unable to express genuine faith was brought to the ground. There is nothing like faith to bring down barriers. Faith can move the highest mountain dividing us one from another. Faith can bridge the dividing sea between us. Faith can cut across cultures, gender, class, and even enemy lines. Why shouldn't believers continue to strive to eliminate those barriers and things in human life that continue to separate us from God and from one another? This presents a clear picture of the result of faith expressed in the Person of Jesus. Faith in Jesus Christ is our key to dealing with our tendency to alienate others. It is this man's faith expressed in Jesus that becomes the basis of breaking down long held stereotypical traditions. The man's faith gave him entrance into the very heart of God's Son.

"Everything" said Jesus, is possible to those who have faith (Mark 9:23). We, as Christians, are called to have faith, not just for our own salvation but for the salvation of this world; we are called to believe that Jesus has the power and the authority to make things whole. By faith, we could have all that we need then move beyond ourselves reaching and touching God for someone other than ourselves. This is good news—that faith in Jesus can break boundaries.

Finally, Jesus uses the centurion's faith to teach a lesson which His life illustrates. He says, "And I say unto you, That many shall come from the east and west, and shall sit down with Abraham, and Isaac, and Jacob, in the kingdom of heaven" (v. 11).

Through Jesus Christ, the kingdom of heaven has come down to everyone. Everyone who comes to Jesus, whether they be from the east or from the west, from the south or from the north, will sit in the divine reign with God. This is the good news that breaks down boundaries.

Chapter Eight

EQUIPPED FOR VICTORY

BASED ON MATTHEW 4:1-11

Matthew 4:1-11

Then was Jesus led up of the Spirit into the wilderness to be tempted of the devil. ² *And when he had fasted forty days and forty nights, he was afterward an hungered.* ³ *And when the tempter came to him, he said, If thou be the Son of God, command that these stones be made bread.* ⁴*But he answered and said, It is written, Man shall not live by bread alone, but by every word that proceedeth out of the mouth of God.* ⁵*Then the devil taketh him up into the holy city, and setteth him on a pinnacle of the temple,* ⁶ *nd saith unto him, If thou be the Son of God, cast thyself down: for it is written, He shall give his angels charge concerning thee: and in their hands they shall bear thee up, lest at any time thou dash thy foot against a stone.* ⁷*Jesus said unto him, It is written again, Thou shalt not tempt the Lord thy God.* ⁸*Again, the devil taketh him up into an exceeding high mountain, and sheweth him all the kingdoms of the world, and the glory of them;* ⁹*And saith unto him, All these things will I give thee, if thou wilt fall down and worship me.* ¹⁰*Then saith Jesus unto him, Get thee hence, Satan: for it is written, Thou shalt worship the Lord thy God, and him only shalt thou serve.* ¹¹*Then the devil leaveth him, and, behold, angels came and ministered unto him.*

The following story illustrates the power of the Word. Shanab had been through a rough time. The last three months had been difficult. His wife Andina, whom he loved very much, just became sick. The doctors were at a loss. His son, who was doing well in school, now seemed to be running into trouble with the teacher. Shanab's boss, who always had been very pleasant, turned sour and began to make life at work almost unbearable. All this happened right after he and his family decided that they were going to be more than pew-warmers at church. After the pastor preached last week, the whole family went forward to rededicate their lives to God.

As all these troubles came up one after another in the same week, Andina sat down one evening and began to consider how to deal with this situation. She and Shanab decided they were going to collect articles on the various issues which now assailed their family and share the insights they had gleaned. They prayed together. Shanab and Andina had never seen themselves as "Bible thumpers." As strange as it may seem, however, they did not resolve to read the Scriptures. They read many things; they combed the pages of the Times, Ebony, Jet, Essence, Psychology Today, and other books for insight into their situation and how to deal with it. At church, they held onto every word spoken from the pulpit. One Sunday, the pastor preached from the fourth chapter of Matthew on how Jesus used the Word of God to fight the battles that he encountered. As the minister was speaking, Shanab turned to Andina and said, "Why don't we start studying the Bible together?" To which she replied, "I was just thinking the same thing." They both began to study Scriptures more intensely. Two months later, they were having a conversation and they both expressed how much insight they had gained from the Word of God. Shanab remarked about how contemporary the Word of God seemed to be. Andina shared how she had slowly been using the insights gained from the Scriptures to order her life. Shanab said, "I noticed, and I am so proud of you, and I thank God." The Word of God helped this family gain insight into the will of God for their lives.

In Matthew 4:1-11 we read that after being baptized by John, Jesus is led into the wilderness to be "tempted by the devil." The Greek word translated "tempted" means to test one's character or virtue by enticement to sin. Jesus had to prove His allegiance to do the will of the Father. Satan wanted Him to fail like the Children of Israel failed in the wilderness. Would the Son of God succumb to the temptation of the devil? The fact that the Spirit leads Him into the wilderness suggests that victory is at hand.

We are told that Jesus had been fasting for 40 days and 40

EQUIPPED FOR VICTORY

nights. In the Bible, there are only two other individuals who are said to have fasted for the same amount of time: Moses (Exodus 34:28) and Elijah (1 Kings 19:8). Fasting is defined as "to deny oneself of nourishment for a defined amount of time." The purpose is to enable one to hear the instruction and direction of God more clearly, and to place the appetites of the body in submission. Most of the time, if not always, fasting is associated with communing with God, such as Moses at Mount Sinai and Elijah at Mount Horeb. Matthew does not say that Jesus is praying, but it is implied by the fact that He was led by the Spirit into this period of testing.

The devil appears at the apex of Jesus' physical weakness. Verse 2 says He was "hungry." His body craved nourishment. So the tempter challenges Jesus to turn a stone into bread to satisfy His hunger. Satan tries to get Jesus to cater to His physical cravings—to use His power and authority to fulfill a physical desire. Jesus answered by quoting Deuteronomy 8:3. He, in essence, tells us that the desires of the flesh are not important, but the desires of God are. It is God's Word that takes precedence over everything else. Human beings do not subsist by obeying physical cravings, but they live through the internalization of God's Word.

Since Jesus used Scripture to combat the tempter, the tempter now decides to use Scripture out of context to cause Jesus to falter. The second temptation calls upon Jesus to test God's promise in Psalms 91:11-12. This promise ensures protection from an enemy or some mishap. The tempter suggests that Jesus should test God's promise by throwing Himself off the pinnacle of the temple to see if the angels will catch Him. Jesus replied by quoting Deuteronomy 6:16, which says that God is not to be tested.

In the third and last temptation, the tempter offers Jesus the kingdoms of the earth in exchange for Jesus' worship and allegiance. Jesus again quotes Scripture, Deuteronomy 6:13. He states that God alone should receive worship and allegiance. After this, the tempter leaves Jesus and He is ministered to by the angels. By passing these tests, Jesus shows that He is sold out to fulfill the will of God. There is no place for self-gratification, aggrandizement, or selfish greed. Jesus has become the example of the perfect servant of God. He is now able to go and call others to discipleship—to follow Him as He fulfills His mission to bring glory to God and to give Himself as a living sacrifice.

What Is the Word?
The Word As A Person

In Matthew 4:1-11, the key instrument is the Word. It should be remembered that a word in the original Hebrew and Greek was not merely sound, but was the expression of the inner disposition of the speaker. Thus when the word is used, it is inclusive of the thought from which the word is born. So a person's word is really representative of the person. Because the word is the expression of the thought of the person, so what someone says really represents her or him. Within the Scriptures there are, indeed, three expressions of the Word. For Christians, the Word is primarily a Person. This idea is expressed in the Gospel of John 1:1-14 where the Word of God is equated with God and, in fact, with the Person of Jesus the Messiah; Jesus as the Word of God who is God. There is no Christian thought, preaching, teaching, or sharing, that is possible without this personal Word of God. In Matthew chapter 4, we encounter two modes of the Word of God. First, we encounter Jesus as the Word of God. Then we find Jesus using the Word of God, which is Scripture.

Jesus is the Word of God which communicates salvation to us. If the Word of God is a Person, then it is also relational. Jesus is the Word which relates human beings to God. All other definitions of the Word must find their grounding in Jesus as the personal Word of God spoken from eternity and history to humanity. This means that listening faithfully and acknowledging Jesus as the Word of God should be a priority for every believer. As the Word of God, Jesus is the activator of human faith. For the nature and activity to make sense to any of us, we must pay attention to Jesus as what theologians call the "Divine-Word-Event."

The Greek word *logos* that is used by John to describe Jesus as the second Person of the Trinity signifies the speech and wisdom of God. Jesus is the divine speech who arranges and orders all things. The Apostle John puts it this way, "by him all things were created, and without him nothing was made that was made" (John 1:3). When you see beauty, know that it is the Word that formed it. As the personal Word of God, Jesus embodies the excellence and the majesty of divine thought and expression.

The Word As Written

Ordinarily, when Christians refer to the Word of God they mean the Bible. In the written Word of God, God has revealed who He is in a special way. Therefore, the Bible could actually be called the "Book of the Acts of God" because it contains what God has done and will do for the world. This Book reveals God's call, God's deliverance, God's covenant relationship, God's judgment, God's restoration, and God's eternal reign. Several themes within the Bible show it to be the Word of God, but the one key theme is the theme of salvation. Throughout the Bible, we see that God is Saviour.

The Bible is not just a history book, though it speaks of historical events. However, the record of these historical events was written by inspiration from God. Peter puts it this way, "Knowing this first, that no prophecy of scripture is of any private interpretation. For the prophecy came not in old times by the will of man: but holy men of God spake as they were moved by the Holy Ghost" (2 Peter 1:20-21). Paul when writing to Timothy in the second letter states, "All scripture is given by the inspiration of God, and is profitable for doctrine, for reproof, for correction, for instruction in righteousness: that the man of God may be perfect, thoroughly furnished unto all good works" (2 Timothy 3:16-17). According to the scriptural records themselves, the content of this special Book was inspired by God.

Anyone who desires to walk with God and have intimate knowledge of God's ways must know the Holy Scriptures. In the Scriptures, divine truths are revealed, which if we learn them, guide us truly. For the Christian, all our grounding must come from what God says to us in the Scriptures. We must not allow the Word of God to sit somewhere and gather dust, or we will be like someone who has great treasures but seldom uses them. As people who believe that our destiny is eternal, the Bible can guide us into a deeper understanding of what it means to have this life.

There is something in the Scriptures which is suitable for every situation we face. Oh, that we may love our Bibles more, and read them often! Then shall we find benefit, and gain the lasting happiness promised therein by faith in our Lord Jesus Christ, who is the main subject of both testaments. We best oppose error by possessing a solid knowledge of the Word of truth, and the greatest kindness we can show children is to teach them the Scriptures early.

What Can the Word Do?

In Matthew 4:1-11, we find Jesus (who is the personal Word of God) citing the written Word of God. This tells us that the Word of God serves a certain function in the lives of those who believe.

First, it serves as our defense against the attack of the enemy. Look at how many times Jesus responded to the tempter with the words, "It is written." If, as Paul says to Timothy, all Scripture is God-inspired, then the Holy Spirit is at work in the Word. When Jesus cites the written Word, He activates the power of the Holy Spirit. Many times we read in Scripture that the Word is a sword. When Jesus faced the devil in spiritual warfare in Matthew chapter 4, He used the Word.

Second, the Word of God can be helpful for interpreting life's experiences. Many times in Scripture, the Prophets cite the Law of Moses to interpret what God was doing in their time (Ezra 3:2; Daniel 9:11-13). The New Testament is particularly full of these examples (Matthew 1:22; 2:5, 15, 17; Mark 7:10).

Third, the Word of God functions to give us a right understanding of God's nature. Scripture places a heavy premium on having a good understanding of God. A good understanding

of God is important for a right worship of God. That is precisely why the Decalogue begins with "Hear O Israel, the Lord
your God is One God" then proceeds to say, "Love the Lord
your God with all your heart and with all your soul and with all
your strength" (Deuteronomy 6:4-5). In the Bible we discover
how faithful women and men have worshiped God. We also
find the kinds of worship that are not acceptable to God. The
Word of God functions to enlighten our soul. The psalmist was
clear about this when he said, "The entrance of the word gives
light" (Psalm 119:130). The Word of God helps us to act right.

"Thy word have I hidden in my heart that I might not sin against thee," says the psalmist (Psalm 119:11).

Fourth, the Word functions as a corrective to our human tendency to embrace the things that wound the heart of God. Thus Paul tells us that it is profitable for instruction (2 Timothy 3:16). Over and over again, we hear Jesus refer to the Scripture as a way to correct the tendency of His audience to misrepresent God and God's work in the world. (See Matthew 21:42; 22:31-32, 26:54-56; Mark 12:24.)

How Can the Word of God Become Effective in Your Life?

First, for the Word to be effective in our lives, we must know the Word of God. One way to get to know the Word of God is to read it. Jesus practiced reading the Scriptures. We know this from the way He quoted them. We are also told in Scripture that it was His custom to read the Scriptures in public. If you have had the privilege of learning to read and write, there is no reason why you should not be reading the Scriptures to find out what treasures God has laid in store for you in his Word.

Second, we need to hear the Word of God. Many times in the Bible we read the phrase: "Hear the word of the Lord." The Bible says, "Faith cometh by hearing and hearing by the word of God" (Romans 10:17). Listening to the spoken Word of God can produce faith (Romans 10:14). As the Word of God enters into our being, it has the power to lead us to the point of salvation (Romans 1:16). Be encouraged to make listening to the Word of God a top priority in your life. When you hear the Word preached, ask yourself what God's Word is for you in the message instead of sitting in judgment on how well the preacher or the speaker presents the Word. We must learn to listen with humility, however, this does not mean that we listen without discernment. We must listen with discernment, for whatever word we hear is the word by which we shall be judged. In the story of the rich man and Lazarus, there is a strong warning that if we do not listen to those who bring the message to us everyday, we set ourselves up for condemnation (Luke 16:19-31). The key to receiving the power inherent in the Word is found in hearing. But those who speak the Word must do so in truth. Even when you witness to the Word of God, you must do so in truth (Jeremiah 23:28-29; 2 Corinthians 2:17). Because hearing the Word is so important, Jesus warns us to be careful how we hear (Mark 4:24). The Word is that seed that bears righteous fruit (Luke 8:11). It will help you cut through the morass of human mess and give you direction in confusion (Hebrews 4:12-13).

Third, we must make the Word which we have read or heard such an important part of our lives that it becomes a part of our thinking process. This is called "meditating upon the Word." Some people take the time to memorize the portions of the Scripture from which God is speaking to them. Although some people are unable to memorize Scripture word for word, it is still important to develop a way of remembering the Word of God to experience its effectiveness in your every-day life. Another way to make it a part of your life is to share findings from the Word of God with others. The formation of our thinking process by the Word of God is vital for our maturity of faith. In the Hebrew testament, the most frequently used word is "thought" (Hebrew *machashebheth,* from the verb *chashabh,* "to think"), which refers to the ability to have firm purpose. As Christians, our purpose must be formed by the Word of God. In the New Testament, the word *dialogismos* (Matthew 15:19; 1 Corinthians 3:20) translated as the word "dialogue" refers to the inner reasoning or deliberation that one has with oneself. Similarly, The Old Testament often translates the verb amar, "to say," to mean what one says to himself; and hence implies a definite and clearly formulated decision or purpose (Genesis 20:11; Numbers 24:4; Ruth 4:4). This meaning is illustrated by the change made in Esther 6:6 of the Revised Standard Version (British and American) where "thought in his heart" from the King James Version becomes "said in his heart."

Fourth, do not be afraid to apply the Word of God in your life's contexts. There is really no greater way to make God's

Word part of our life than to practice it daily. When we study or listen and interact with the Word of God, it helps us to gain insight on our situation and to cope with it in realistic ways. Our spiritual health advances as we progress in the knowledge of God's Word. We can also apply it in our relationships with those around us. As we study the Word of God, we develop an inner stability which allows us to maintain our integrity through the various crises that we face in this world. Many people attempt to deal with life's stresses by getting involved in all sorts activities in an effort to ease the pain. The Christian, however, has a standard source which is the Word of God. Many of our problems stem from spiritual imbalance, therefore we must find the solution in the spiritual principles inherent in the Word of God. But in doing so, we must be careful not to use the Word of God as an excuse for not doing the things we need to do to maintain overall sound lifestyles. For example, one should not quit a job just because God's Word says He will provide all of our needs according to His riches and glory. There is a factor of realism in the Word of God which will not excuse us if we choose to ignore the simple guidelines for life which God has laid out. But when all is said and done, the Word of God is still the instrument for development toward the practice of a life of victory.

By making the Word your partner in your everyday life, you will blossom into the beautiful creature that God created you to be. The Word of God is available for you. It is your weapon for the spiritual battle you must wage in this world. It is your light for the journey which we all must travel as we pass through the valleys of life. Only by immersing ourselves in all the manifestations of the divine Word, can we keep in step with the Master—Jesus who is the Messiah.

Chapter Nine

PREPARATION FOR ULTIMATE VICTORY

BASED ON MATTHEW 24:45-51; 25:1-13

Matthew 24:45-51

Who then is a faithful and wise servant, whom his lord hath made ruler over his household, to give them meat in due season? ⁴⁶ Blessed is that servant, whom his lord when he cometh shall find so doing. ⁴⁷ Verily I say unto you, That he shall make him ruler over all his goods. ⁴⁸ But and if that evil servant shall say in his heart, My lord delayeth his coming; ⁴⁹ And shall begin to smite his fellow servants, and to eat and drink with the drunken; ⁵⁰ The lord of that servant shall come in a day when he looketh not for him, and in an hour that he is not aware of, ⁵¹ And shall cut him asunder, and appoint him his portion with the hypocrites: there shall be weeping and gnashing of teeth.

Matthew 25:1-13

Then shall the kingdom of heaven be likened unto ten virgins, which took their lamps, and went forth to meet the bridegroom. ²And five of them were wise, and five were foolish. ³They that were foolish took their lamps, and took no oil with them: 4 But the wise took oil in their vessels with their lamps. ⁵While the bridegroom tarried, they all slumbered and slept. ⁶And at midnight there was a cry made, Behold, the bridegroom cometh; go ye out to meet him. ⁷Then all those virgins arose, and trimmed their lamps. ⁸And the foolish said unto the wise, Give us of your oil; for our lamps are gone out. ⁹ But the wise answered, saying, Not so; lest there be not enough for us and you: but go ye rather to them that sell, and buy for yourselves. ¹⁰And while they went to buy, the bridegroom came; and they that were ready went in with him to the marriage: and the door was shut. ¹¹Afterward came also the other virgins, saying, Lord, Lord, open to us. ¹²But he *answered and said, Verily I say unto you, I know you not. ¹³Watch therefore, for ye know neither the day nor the hour wherein the Son of man cometh.*

Victory belongs to the watchful but defeat shall visit the slothful. The need for watchfulness and vigilance is captured in a story taken from the American Revolutionary War that illustrates how tragedy can result from procrastination. Colonel Rahl, commander of the British troops in Trenton, New Jersey, was playing cards when a courier brought an urgent message stating that General George Washington was crossing the Delaware River. Rahl put the message in his pocket and didn't bother to read it until the game was finished. Then, realizing the seriousness of the situation, he hurriedly tried to rally his men to meet the coming attack, but his procrastination was his undoing. He and many of his men were killed, and the rest of the regiment were captured. Nolbert Quayle said, "Only a few minutes of delay cost him his life, his honor, and the liberty of his soldiers. Earth's history is strewn with the wrecks of half-finished plans and unexecuted resolutions. 'Tomorrow' is the excuse of the lazy and refuge of the incompetent." This need for vigilance is also affirmed in Jesus's statement, "Watch therefore, for ye know neither the day nor the hour wherein the Son of man cometh" (Matthew 25:13).

As an American citizen, one may have heard this story from General Washington's perspective. However, it is clear that the outcome of that battle may have been different had Colonel Rahl and his men been prepared and anticipated the approach of General Washington and his troops. Procrastination cost the British, perhaps a victory, or at least a fair fight.

This parable like the other parables in the Scripture provides a vision of the mode of living demanded of those who are members of God's kingdom. We are meant to align our lives and actions with the divine ideals set for us in Holy Writ. The examples within this text extend themselves into our daily lives and disclose the path we should choose for ourselves. The stories of Jesus are linked with the heritage of the prophetic parables in the Old Testament (Isaiah 28:23-29; 5:1-7; 1 Kings 20:39-43; Ecclesiastes 9:13-16; 2 Samuel 12:1-4).

Many of the parables grew out of conflicts in which Jesus answered His religious critics. These parables, usually intended for Pharisees and sinners simultaneously, expose and extol. Jesus exposed the self-righteousness of His critics and extolled the kingdom of God. When John the Baptist was accused of being too serious and Jesus of being too frivolous, Jesus came back with the parable of the playing children (Matthew 11:16-19; Luke 7:31-35) to expose the inconsistency of the criticism. In one of His most famous parables, He extolled the forgiving love of the father and exposed the hostile criticism of the unforgiving elder brother (Luke 15:11-32). In fact, Jesus interpreted His ministry and its place in the history of salvation by means of a parable. The parables are not merely clever stories but a proclamation of the Gospel. The listener must respond and is invited to make a decision about the kingdom and the King. The parable of the wicked tenants (Mark 12:1-12) represents a blatant confrontation.

These stories got Jesus in trouble as He made veiled claims of kingliness and exposed hypocrisy in the religious hierarchy. One of the reasons they crucified Jesus was because of His challenging parables and the claims of His kingdom. Some of the stories carry a pastoral and others a prophetic relevance. The parable of the mustard seed (Matthew 13:31-32) speaks pastorally about ending despair, and the parable of the persistent widow (Luke 18:1-8) encourages us to never give up. The parable of the barren fig tree (Luke 13:6-9) speaks prophetically concerning national priorities; the parable of the wicked tenants (Luke 20:9-19) accosts arrogant religious leaders; and the parable of the rich fool (Luke 12:16-21) confronts false confidence in materialism. Through the parable of the Pharisee and the tax collector (Luke 18:9-14), grace reigns down on two people praying in the temple, and we see that appearances are deceiving. Grace shines on worship, and revelation happens! (Adapted from "Parables" by Peter Rhea Jones, in *Homan's Bible Dictionary for Windows*, Version 1.0, Parsons Technology, 1994.)

The text here occurs as Jesus leaves the temple, having upset religious practitioners. His disciples, like many, begin to get preoccupied with the outward appearance of the temple. They were caught in the temporal fixtures of the temple. In the midst of their romantic religious reverie, Jesus makes a startling comment. He predicts the ultimate physical and symbolic ruin of the temple. This surprises the disciples and is, to them, inconceivable; the presence of the temple was central to Jewish worship customs. Yet Jesus, having their rapt attention, seizes this teachable moment to warn the disciples of an influx of false prophets. He foretells extreme trouble and persecution of Christians, and exhorts them to prepare and remain prepared for His return. The disciples ask Jesus two questions which set the stage for the events to follow: (1) When would the Temple be destroyed; and (2) what would be the signs of His return? Jesus answered them: (1) The temple would be destroyed in their lifetime; (2) a great cosmic procession would make His return visible and obvious to all on Earth. There are several interpretations of the events shown in this text.

Jesus told a parable about faithful and unfaithful servants and also the story of the ten virgins to illustrate the importance of being prepared for His return. This parable could be considered a clarion call to church leaders to prepare for His return. But it relates to all of us as servants of the Lord. These servants are the overseers of all of the household servants in the master's absence. Although both are aware the master is gone and will eventually return, the contrast of how they fulfill their tasks are vivid. The wise servant deals judiciously and consistently with the other servants in attending to the master's business. He is least concerned for the time of the master's return, but attends instead to his call and his commitment of service.

The contrast is not so much in the act of foolishness versus the act of wisdom, but rather the wisdom and foolishness is inherent in the demonstration of faithfulness or the lack of it. When we list the characteristics of those who are prepared to win ultimate victory we may list faithfulness at the top of the list. Faithfulness is the first requirement for anyone who intends to live a victorious life and to partake in ultimate victory when the Master comes. Faithfulness is the bedrock of Christianity. Faithfulness is the foundation of Christian values; we cannot receive what God has for us without this one core principle.

Faithfulness raises even the weak and mediocre to a level that even the most powerful who lack it may never attain. It takes all that we are to be faithful—our mind, our strength and our emotions. Faithfulness is not meant to be a group phenomenon; is our inner resolve to stay connected to God even in the face of loss. By being faithful we ascend with our soul to those things which God has promised. Thus faithfulness is grounded in the hopeful expectation. As faithful servants, we remain at our divinely ordained workplace that God has entrusted unto us. We are entrusted with God's words and with the hearts of our brothers and sisters as we execute the commands of the Lord.

Faith holds a connection to work. And it is the characteristic that reveals our likeness to God, for God is faithful. Faithfulness demands that we be persons worthy of divine trust and that we be tenacious in holding onto that which is greater than ourselves. We fail in faithfulness if we suppose, as some do, that it proceeds from ourselves. The faithful servant is convinced of the power of God to sustain in all circumstances as he seeks to remain in the center of the divine will, never allowing enfeebling negativity or unbelief to overtake as he operates within the divine. Admitting faith in the face of obvious difficulty may seem an impossibility for some, but it is faith which grants ultimate victory. Faith is connected to confidence, and our confidence is not in ourselves but in God.

Faithfulness demands that if because of the name of our God we face condemnation by the world, even by members of the Church who would prefer that we be mediocre in our faith, that we remain steadfast. As soldiers of the Cross our victory is only assured if we do not seek the easy way out and if we take care to hold onto the power which God has placed within us. Faithfulness belongs to those who have become repositories of the Holy Spirit, who have his continuous illumination. The faithful can only remain so if they, by the power of the Holy

Spirit, keep in mind the glorious Word of God. The incorruptible crown, and the testimony of the Lord and the eternal fellowship in his presence is afforded not to those who give up in the middle but to those who remain faithful unto death. Every day I encourage my soul to remain faithful. You are encouraged by Jesus Christ the Bishop to remain faithful. Do not lose your resolve in the face of the world's fickleness. Remain faithful. Do not get weary as you labor in a world in which spiritual laziness has become the order of the day. Remain faithful. If per chance your faith slips, set yourself again on the road to faithful stewardship.

In the text faithfulness is illustrated by the care which the servant shows to his fellow servants. It may be demonstrated mainly in church attendance or in singing in the choir. But in this text it is measured by how one cares for one's fellow servants. Faithfulness does not demand us to attempt to do that which is beyond our ability. The reason many give up is that they attempt to work beyond their giftedness. But faithfulness can be maintained if we minister according to the proportion of ability instilled within us. Not everyone can ransom the kidnapped, build a church or go to ends of the world to help the needy. God requires only that we remain diligent at our call station. We will be blessed, and will attain ultimate victory with Christ if we remain faithful right where we belong. Faithfulness demands that we care for those who are less fortunate in this world's goods than we are. In fact, Jesus to a would-be follower said, "go sell all your goods and give to the poor, if thou will be perfect." A faithful follower will suffer martyrdom for the ultimate goal of marching victoriously with the King of kings. It is the faithful who care for their fellow servants who are deemed worthy of God. Jesus even made our ability to care the basis of entering into eternal victory with him.

"Come, ye blessed of my Father, inherit the kingdom prepared for you from the foundation of the world. For I was hungry, and ye gave me meat; I was thirsty, and ye gave me drink; I was a stranger, and ye took me in; naked, and ye clothed me; I was sick, and ye visited me; I was in prison, and ye came unto me. Then shall the righteous answer, and say, Lord, when saw we Thee an hungered, and fed Thee? or thirsty, and gave Thee drink? When saw we Thee naked, and clothed Thee? or sick, and visited Thee? When saw we Thee a stranger, and took Thee in? or in prison, and came unto Thee? And He will answer and say unto them, Inasmuch as ye have done it unto one of the least of these my brethren, ye have done it unto me. And these shall go away into life everlasting.

Then shall He say unto them on His left hand, Depart from me, ye cursed, into everlasting fire, prepared for the devil and his angels. For I was hungry, and ye gave me no meat; I was thirsty, and ye gave me no drink; I was a stranger, and ye took me not in; naked, and ye clothed me not; sick, and in prison, and ye visited me not. Then shall they also answer and say, Lord when saw we Thee hungry, or thirsty, or a stranger, or naked, or sick, or in prison, and did not minister unto Thee? Then shall He answer and say unto them, Verily I say unto you, Inasmuch as ye did it not unto one of the least of these, ye did it not to me. And these shall go away unto everlasting punishment" (Matthew 25:45, 46a).

The question which Jesus asks, "who then is that faithful and wise servant whom his master made ruler over his household to give them food in due season?" deals with three issues: faithfulness, wisdom and care. Some are faithful, that is they keep on the task. But some keep on the task and do not know when the task should be changed. They want to keep doing what they have done even when the spirit has left. But faithfulness must be seasoned with wisdom. There are those who are faithful and wise. They know what is required to be done and where to go and how to keep on the task demanded of them, but they fail to consider the weak among them. They trample on others in their faithfulness and wisdom. The word used here is not the word *sophia* but the word *phronimos* from the word *phroneo* which refers to human thoughtfulness, a tendency towards sagacity and discretion. This servant is of a cautious character and tends to watch for the possible outcome. In many cases this cautious orientation may prevent the faithful from moving to action. But being faithful does not mean that we blind ourselves to the seasons of God's movement. Not only does faithfulness demand this cautious practicalism; it demands that we be able to provide what is needed for God's people in due season. The idea here is that one who would be victorious with Jesus ought to grasp the *kairos,* (**kahee-ros**) that is, the divine occasions of providence. Being at the place of our appointed ministry should not blind us to divine opportunity which is meant to lead us to a new vision and action.

Those who are candidates for the ultimate victory with Jesus must also guard their heart from cynicism. The text says, "but if the evil servant shall say in his heart My master is delaying his coming; and begins to beat his fellow servants and to eat and drink with the drunkards." Having a right heart is very important for attaining victory. The contrast between those who will attain ultimate victory and those who will not is a matter of the condition of their heart and how this condition affects their outward action. We must watch our heart when it seems that our reward is not coming as quickly as we anticipated it.

The first step in losing the battle for which God has chosen us to fight is to lose our heart's direction. Conversely then, if we intend to have victory we must cultivate a certain kind of atmosphere in our hearts. First, we seek the Lord in our heart rather than do as this servant did, which is cultivate rebellion. God will reach out to us when we seek Him with our heart—sometimes even when our actions do not measure up. We must set our heart on the way to seeking God as a preliminary step to our victory over the enemies that beset us (2 Chronicles 19:3). "There is, however, some good in you, for you have rid the land of the Asherah poles and have set your heart on seeking God" (2 Chronicles 30:18-19). At another place we read "Although most of the many people who came from Ephraim, Manasseh, Issachar and Zebulun had not purified themselves, yet they ate the Passover, contrary to what was written. But Hezekiah prayed for them, saying, "May the Lord, who is good, pardon everyone who sets his heart on seeking God—the Lord, the God of his fathers—even if he is not clean according to the rules of the sanctuary'" (see 2 Chronicles 30:18, 19, NIV).

For this victory to become ours we must not only begin to seek the Lord but we must train our hearts to hunger for the Lord as we hunger for water and food. We must say with the psalmist:

"My soul yearns, even faints,
for the courts of the Lord;
my heart and my flesh cry out
for the living God" (Psalm 84:2).

For you see we only find our way into the victorious life in God through Jesus Christ if we seek the Lord with all our hearts. There is no halfway house of seeking. What was wrong with the thought process of this servant is that his desire for his master was halfhearted. He gave his heart only as long as the master was near. He gave his heart only as long as he received certain immediate blessings from the master's physical proximity. His heart was not completely surrendered to the cause of the master. It should not have mattered if the master was never coming back; even the memory of the Master should have served to keep his heart in check. But having never committed fully to the master, he now finds it easy to fall prey to his own weakness and to follow the uncommitted crowd. For those who seek to live a victorious life, this seeking of the Lord must be constant. We cannot just seek Him when things are difficult and seek our own glory when things are going well. Neither can we serve Him when things are going well and fail to seek Him when things are going bad. There was the temptation of Job. Recall the enemy's question "does Job serve God for naught?" With the rise of the prosperity gospel, it would seem that many of us serve God mainly for the possibility of prosperity. If that is the case then those who are suffering and turn to all kinds of evil are justified in not seeking God. God forbid. We ought to seek God at all times, in all conditions and in all places. This is how we prepare ourselves to become whom the song writer calls "victors in the midst of strife."

Another problem with this man who ended up losing the battle for which the master had so well prepared him is the lack of joy in his heart. Notice that his life seem tainted with bitterness and anger. How do I know that? The text says he began to beat and manhandle his fellow servants. What else will lead one to this state of heart except that the heart has been poisoned with an absence of joy. Absence of joy is a very dangerous thing. There are at least two factors, I can speculate, that ate away this man's joy. He was not contented to serve the master, he wanted to be the master. This is evident in the way he treated his fellow servants. Also, he could not tolerate happiness in the other servants.

If you want to lose your joy, and thus lose your victory, the easiest way to do so is to spend your life worrying about what you do not have instead of enjoying what you do have. It is also difficult to be joyful when one is busy trying to keep others from being happy. But both of these are a result of a refusal to be content in God and to allow the fact that one has been chosen by the Lord to infuse joy into one's soul. How often we miss our opportunity for joy because we are more concerned about others who seem to have surpassed us; we cannot rejoice for them in God as we could for ourselves. Those who will be victorious then must cultivate a heart of joy. This was David's secret. In spite of all that befell him, he never ceased to cultivate an attitude of joy. In 1 Samuel 2:1 he says, "My heart rejoices in the LORD." In spite of all his trials he had the audacity to say in Psalm 4:7, "You have filled my heart with greater joy than when their grain and new wine abound." The joyful heart is the heart on the way to victory. But this joy is also what God gives to those who are servants. As the word to Isaiah states:

"My servants will sing out of the joy of their hearts, but you will cry out from anguish of heart and wail in brokenness of spirit" (Isaiah 65:14, NIV).

In the final days God promises joy to Ephraim the wayward son. Joy heals us and strengthens us for the battle ahead (Zechariah 10:7).

Righteousness and joy, which is here compared to light, is a gift which is bestowed upon the upright in heart. Thus, to gain victory one must also seek purity of heart. Psalm 51:10: "Create in me a pure heart, O God, and renew a steadfast spirit within me." Psalm 73:1: "Surely God is good to Israel, to those who are pure in heart." Jesus tells us that seed of divine life, and may I say victorious life, will not germinate unless we somehow through the grace of God have a noble and a good heart. We read in Luke 8:15: "But the seed on good soil stands for those with a noble and good heart, who hear the word, retain it, and by persevering produce a crop."

Not only must the victorious cultivate a joyful, upright and pure heart, they must also develop simplicity of heart. This is a heart that is not encumbered with that which is worldly to the extent that the seed of God's victory deposited within it gets choked to death. The victory of the early church is attributed to this simplicity of heart. We are not here speaking of a refusal to understand or to study, which has led many to false theology and moral demise, but the focus here is a balanced perceptive of the world. We read in Acts 2:46: "So continuing daily with one accord in the temple, and breaking bread from house to house, they ate their food with gladness and simplicity of heart."

In addition to this the victor must be sincere. You have probably heard the phrase that "One can be sincerely wrong, though one may be wrong sincerely." Yet there is no substitute for a sincere heart in the battle in which we are engaged. Paul calls us in Ephesians 6:5 to walk in "sincerity of heart." We must not only deal with each other in sincerity of heart. we must draw near to our God with the same, as we read in "let us draw near with a true heart in full assurance of faith, having our hearts sprinkled from an evil conscience and our bodies washed with pure water." But every warrior gets tired and worn out and the battle gets old. When this happens we must seek God for renewal.

The fact that we get tired of the battle is the reason for continually seeking the Lord. Our hearts need renewal and only the Spirit of the Lord can renew us. When Paul says in Ephesians 4:23: "and be renewed in the spirit of your mind," he knows that we are incapable of renewing ourselves. If the spirit of our mind needs renewal, no material entity can do it for us, only spirit can renew spirit. "God is that Spirit" our Lord tells us. The spirit within us being a direct offspring of God can only find its renewal in getting back in touch with God.

But if our hearts becomes unguarded and in the process of service we begin to consider our labor worthless and doubt the intrinsic truth of our Lord's promise, we may be opening ourselves to evil. In this text the servant who loses his ultimate victory reaches this point because he left his heart unprotected. It is very easy to move from a cynical perspective to depravity of action. In fact the word translated as "evil" can mean with the objective of injury. This intent to do harm because we have done good for so long without positive results is not a tendency that infects every one who is in the battle for good. But our quest for victory demands that we turn a deaf ear to the noisome wickedness of cynicism. And this must begin in our heart before thoughts and feelings have been so affected that their connection to positive possibility has been broken. To attain victory, then we are a called to watch what we say in our hearts. Do we feed our heart with the promise of God or we feed it with the idea that delay means that we have been denied?

The one who would have this victory is the one who speaks divine confidence into his soul. We are prepared to win this ultimate victory if we say in our heart the very things that God has said. Cynicism can be tied to our perception of time. This evil servant who loses ultimate victory does so because he saw divine delay mainly in what the Greeks termed *chronizo*, (pronounced **khron-id'-zo**). When we attempt to confine God's promise to temporal chronological processes we often find our own expectations unfulfilled. But those who seek to win this victory must move beyond mere chronology to trusting the God who by this very nature is not bound by the encryption on our watch. We will be victorious because we have set our eyes on eternity, not temporal process. Human delays do not unnerve us and even seemingly divine delays must be viewed in light of God's goodness and care.

What this servant who loses here failed to realized is that the master trusts him, which is why he has placed him ruler of the household. In fact, it is God who should be concerned if there is a delay and not the servant. To interpret delay as abandonment is to ignore the very faithfulness of God. Cynicism, which is often the giving up on the possibility of positive outcome, may lead one to harshly respond to those who relate to him. We must not take out our frustration with divine process on our brothers and sisters. He that is eager for this victory cares about those who are committed to her or him.

Furthermore, this orientation to victory demands that we not lose our senses by wantonly indulging in the faithless action of the world. It demands carefulness on our part. We must care for ourselves and our relationships. Living in sobriety does not have so much to do with not drinking as it does with not losing one's sense of the divine because of the things we see in the material world. The cynic may have seen how poorly one person treated another, and now they are sure that it impossible to relate to another human being. They go about encouraging others to disregard relationships. It is sometimes easy just to join the company of the despairing and to engage with the miserable in a continuous dirge. But she that seeks to have victory not only replaces fear with faith but allows the spirit to illuminate her senses and must never forget the first Psalm.

"Blessed *is* the man that walketh not in the counsel of the ungodly, nor standeth in the way of sinners, nor sitteth in the seat of the scornful. ²But his delight is in the law of the Lord; and in his law doth he meditate day and night. ³And he shall be like a tree planted by the rivers of water, that bringeth forth his fruit in his season; his leaf also shall not wither; and whatsoever he doeth shall prosper. ⁴The ungodly are not so: but *are* like the chaff which the wind driveth away. ⁵Therefore the ungodly shall not stand in the judgment, nor sinners in the congregation of the righteous. 6 For the Lord knoweth the way of the righteous: but the way of the ungodly shall perish" (Psalm 1:6).

Another critical element in attaining victory with Jesus is

watchfulness. The attainment of this victory requires watchfulness. This watchfulness is not pointed out in the text that deal with the servant but is more pronounced in the second text underscored in the text of the ten virgins. These maidens are called "virgins" in the KJV and the NIV, "bridesmaids" in the LB, and "maidens" in the RSV. Each of these terms is associated with the Greek word *parthenos,* which means chaste and an unmarried daughter. In a parable about five wise and five foolish maidens, Jesus emphasizes being prepared for His return. Lest believers conclude that He is only interested in leaders' responsibility for readiness, Jesus now turns His attention away from the leaders' to the individual's responsibility to prepare for His return. The setting of this parable is of a wedding.

A wedding was the greatest festival of this culture; the people understood the significance of being a bridesmaid. When a wedding was going on, all other business stopped, and the entire town focused on the wedding and the wedding party. All eyes were on the maidens, those betrothed to a bridegroom. This betrothal indicates that the bridegroom was not seen; however, his return was expected. It is common knowledge to the bridesmaids that the bridegroom is coming. The bridesmaids, however, differed in how they perceived their roles. Five prepared for his return, expecting him at any moment, and five figured he would return eventually, but that his arrival was not imminent. Five of the bridesmaids came with extra oil for their lamps, and five did not. When the bridegroom came later than expected, the foolish bridesmaids had to go buy more oil. Five of them made provision above and beyond their need, while the other five figured that when he returned, they would have time to get ready. Jesus' parable stresses the individual responsibility to be prepared.

While the five bridesmaids were gone, the bridegroom came, and those who were ready went with him to the marriage feast and the door was closed. No one can explain the bridegroom's delay, or Christ's delay, in returning. What is important to the Church, however, is that knowledge of the time of His return is not sufficient for entrance into His eternal reign. This knowledge must be accompanied with preparation. All of the bridesmaids knew the bridegroom would come for them, but the wise ones prepared for his return before they went to sleep. Jesus points out that even though all bridesmaids brought lamps, expecting a night return, five of them did not expect His return that night.

All of the bridesmaids grew tired of waiting and went to sleep, which in itself is no offense. Sleep, or rest, was needed by the physical body. The difference, however, was that five of the bridesmaids took care of business before going to bed.

At midnight there was a great awakening. Five of the bridesmaids awoke with great joy and five with great sadness. The prepared bridesmaids were joined with the bridegroom and the wedding festivities began. The foolish bridesmaids tried to get oil from the wise bridesmaids, but were refused. Their refusal, as first glance, may seem harsh and indifferent. However, it was the wisest decision made. With the wedding taking place at night, if they had shared their oil, there would not have been enough oil and light to last throughout the festivities. The wise bridesmaids could not share their preparedness. Here Jesus stresses the importance to each of us to prepare for His return. It is not enough to live in the here and now; it is equally important to prepare for the hereafter. By the time the five bridesmaids returned to the place of the wedding festival, the door was shut; the opportunity to reign as maidens was closed to them. Tragically, the bridegroom would not acknowledge a bridesmaid who did not prepare for his return while there was time. Jesus declared that one should be ready at all times because no one knows the time of His return. This is an exhortation to focus on a Christian lifestyle, not cultural legalism, while awaiting the return of the Lord.

We must also be watchful, which demands more effort than passively waiting. Like the wise women more effort must be exerted so that our lamp can be kept burning. As true soldiers our belt must not be unloosed. Our watchfulness points out our very readiness. We may say we are watchful, ready and all geared up, but we must also be inwardly ready and willing to go the extra mile to do that little extra which may result in victory.

I once heard a businessman say that he got successful simply by doing a little bit more than was expected. How can we obtain ultimate victory if all we do is mediocre work? If all we want to do is the Sunday morning gig but will not carry an extra load for the kingdom, how can we win the victory which has been promised to us? While we cannot gain the kingdom by works alone, take note that the master expected the servant to work while he was out. In fact He says "blessed is that servant, whom the master when he comes will find so doing."

One day He will come with victory in hand, so here the question is when He comes, will He find that you have been doing? Will He find that you have made a little extra effort? He has promised us the victory both in our situation now and in the ultimate, and one day we shall see things which our souls have not even dreamt about. Then only our faithfulness and our willingness to go the extra mile for our God will count. Without faithfulness how will our churches profit? Many say that we are in the last days. We have heard that in the last days false prophets and corrupters shall be multiplied. We have also read that there shall be wolves who have given up being sheep. Many of these people will be those who no longer believe that God will give victory, and their former love will have turned into hate. But we know that we will be victorious only if we will remain faithful no matter what happens. If we will endure in our faith, we shall be saved.

How can we remain faithful to gain victory when Jesus comes? How can we keep our hearts from straying? The truth is that we cannot do these things on our own. For this, Jesus promised us the Holy Spirit. As you probably are aware, the oil of the virgins is a symbol of the Holy Spirit. Being filled with the Spirit is so vital that after Jesus' resurrection, He remained on Earth 40 days and was seen by the apostles and other followers. He also spoke with them concerning the kingdom of God and with that instructed regarding the promise of the Father, which was prophesied by Joel (Joel 2:28-29).

We know that the Prophet Joel had predicted the day when God was going to pour out His Holy Spirit upon all flesh—that is, on all who called upon the name of Jesus Christ, repented of their sins, and surrendered their lives to His Lordship. The outpouring of the Holy Spirit would enable God's people to flow in the Spirit's power in order to witness for Christ, win the lost to Him, and teach them how to observe all that He had commanded. The problem with both the servant and the unprepared virgins is the lack of something in their hearts. If I may take hermeneutical license, I would suggest that they were filled with themselves or the world and not with the Spirit of the Messiah. No matter what your understanding of the Holy Spirit may be, we as Christians cannot overcome without being empowered by the Holy Spirit. In fact, a major sign of the Messiah, according to John the Baptist, is that He will be One who baptizes His followers with fire and the Holy Spirit (John 1:33).

In Greek, the word "power" is *dunamis* from which we get our English word "dynamite." The power in the life of a believer is not just strength to accomplish things in our own ability, but in the supernatural flow and power of God through His Holy Spirit. The Book of Acts (as well as the Gospel of Luke), teaches us that the Holy Spirit's power in the life of a believer includes the authority in the name of Jesus to drive out evil spirits and heal the sick. In fact, these two signs were to accompany the proclamation of the Gospel (Luke 4:14, 36; Acts 6:8; 8:4-8; 14:13). We must understand why God promised to give us the gift of the Holy Spirit. God has called us to be effective witnesses for Christ and not just pew-warmers in the church.

One of the definitions for "witness" literally means one who may suffer persecution and death for the cause of Christ. Is there any wonder we need the power of the Holy Spirit? But more than that, it is the Holy Spirit who provides us with the stamina needed to stay the course through delays, road blocks, dry spells and even threats to our lives.

The servant in the first text had no patience. He could not wait for the master. He gave up. The ability to wait and to do so patiently is one of the gifts of the Holy Spirit. Jesus Himself says "he that endured to the end shall be saved." This endurance, this long suffering, this patience and radical tenacity is not ours by our human nature but it is fruit born of the Holy Spirit. If we will obtain the victory promised we must be filled with the Holy Spirit. The Holy Spirit will do several things.

The Holy Spirit gives us miraculous signs and wonders so that the world may know about Jesus Christ. The Holy Spirit gives us grace to live godly lives and overcome sin in the midst of a perverse and crooked generation. The Holy Spirit gives us the desire to love, honor, and submit to the Lordship of Jesus Christ. The Holy Spirit will witness to righteousness and truth by bringing conviction of sin in the lives of both Christians and unbelievers (John 16:8-10, 13). The Holy Spirit will help us to become more like Jesus Christ in everything we do. Victory comes to us through obedience. Again the failure of both the servant and the five foolish virgins rests on the lack of obedience. One of the things that Jesus promised was power to walk in the will of God.

The presence of the Holy Spirit in our life is the presence of power working in us and through us to do God's will. Today, the church needs the power of the Holy Spirit to fulfill the responsibility placed upon it by the Lord Jesus Christ in these last days. The onslaught of disobedience in the church based on a false sense of independence really has made the church less victorious than she would have been if she remained obedient. But true victory cannot come without obedience. The Holy Spirit is also the spirit of prayer. The Holy Spirit will not come until we pray and when that Spirit comes we are moved to pray. However, like the early disciples, we must be in our "Upper Room" praying fervently that the power of the Holy Spirit will be evident in our lives as well as the corporate life of the church (Acts 2:14). Since Jesus was a man of prayer (Luke 3:21), we too must pray for God's blessings, power, and the manifestation of His promises in our lives. Jesus encouraged His followers to "tarry" in the city of Jerusalem. They weren't there to have a potluck supper or a fashion show.

Jesus wanted them to be on one accord, praying and seeking God for the promise. The watchfulness which Jesus commanded of both the servant and the virgins in the parable has all along been understood by the church to imply tarrying in prayer. There are many things that can only be accomplished in God's kingdom with persistent and fervent prayer (2 Chronicles 7:14). Jesus also affirms the power of prayer in the lives of New Testament believers today. Thus, the eleven disciples "with the women, and Mary the mother of Jesus and . . . . His brethren" (v. 14) were faithful and committed to fervent prayer in the Upper Room until God's power was made available to them. Through the grace of God, commitment to unity, prayer, and obedience to God's Word, we too can receive the promised power of the Holy Spirit to be effective in the work of Christ just as His disciples were. If we will be a victorious church, triumphantly marching through this world by the power of the Lord we must remain faithful, watch our hearts, be obedient and tarry in the presence of the Lord—in the final analysis, we must be filled with the Spirit.